*The End of
Democracy?*

Regan Arts.

First Regan Arts paperback edition, 2020.
ISBN 978-1-68245-150-2

Library of Congress Control Number: 2020943859

Cover design by *Ariana Losch and M. Marotta Zarba*
Interior design by *Olivier Darbonville*
Cover: vintage Soviet socialist propaganda illustration by *drante/iStock*

Printed in the United States of America
10 9 8 7 6 5 4 3 2 1

Also by Douglas E. Schoen

*Russia and China
on the Rise,
America in Retreat*

DOUGLAS E. SCHOEN

Regan Arts.

NY | LA

Contents

Virus of Lies, Virus of Truth

EMPTY STREETS IN THE WORLD'S GREAT CITIES. BOARD-ed-up storefronts. "Closed" signs in restaurant win-dows. Rider-less subway trains. Masked people, where people can be seen.

Grim scenes from Italian hospitals: hallways crowded with sick patients on gurneys, not all of whom will receive treatment. Nurses and doctors, exhausted, some in tears and supporting one another, outnumbered by those who need their care. They must make decisions about which patients can be saved and which can be merely "made comfortable." Around the world, other countries dread the Italian scenario, in which stress on hospital capacity leads to wartime-like triage operations and—though no one dares quite say it—bodies in the streets.

Fortunately, this scenario does not play out elsewhere, though in New York, hospitals spend anxious weeks with crushes of sick patients, and worries mount that the city will not have the resources needed to treat them all. Eventually, New

York succeeds in "flattening the curve," as the saying goes. Hospitals do not turn away the sick; people do not die in Manhattan streets. But the Manhattan streets are empty of walkers, devoid of commerce, and paralyzed by fear.

The global economy sputters to a near-total halt. The American economy, still the world's great engine of commerce, essentially shuts itself down. Hundreds of millions of people around the world "shelter in place," staying home instead of going out to eat or shop or entertain themselves. Workplaces close. Those whose jobs can be done remotely "work from home," to avoid coming into contact with others. Those whose jobs demand on-site presence—millions of people—lose their jobs, as the business that employ them quickly fold up, unable to sustain a total loss of revenue that stretches from days to weeks to months.

And all along, the lingering questions: how much worse will it get? How many more will die? And how quickly can a treatment be found?

This was the world in March and April 2020: something like a surrealist nightmare, with scenes such as these that would previously have been regarded as the material for dystopian science-fiction novels or disaster films, like *Contagion*. The novel coronavirus, official name Covid-19, was ravaging people and nations everywhere in the most consequential global pandemic since the 1918 influenza. By early August 2020, the new respiratory illness, originating in China, had spread around the world, causing 18.5 million infections and more than 700,000 deaths. In the United States, the numbers were 4.7 million cases and more than 150,000 deaths. The numbers continue to rise.

Economically, too, the numbers are staggering, especially in the United States, where nearly 50 million people have filed for unemployment benefits. Already, the federal government in Washington has unleashed $1.8 trillion in relief, in the form of the CARES Act—a figure more than double the American Recovery and Reinvestment Act of 2009 (commonly referred to as "the stimulus"), passed in the wake of the financial crisis and the Great Recession—and more than half of total 2019 federal revenues.[1] Only time will tell how many businesses have gone under for good, how many millions have joined the permanent ranks of the jobless, and how much in total national wealth has been wiped out by the cessation of activity imposed by lockdowns, shutdowns, and slowdowns all around the United States.

Europe has been hit hard, too. The injunction to "not become another Italy" speaks for itself. Though their total deaths are fewer, Great Britain, France, and most other nations have virus mortality rates considerably worse than that of the U.S. With the grim logic it imposes of isolation and limited contact, the virus might well demolish what remains of the European dream of unity and integration—a dream already threatened by the departure of Britain from the E.U. and years of economic turbulence, amid rising populist and nationalist movements.

Nonetheless, the impact of the coronavirus on the United States has been more transformative than anywhere else. The United States has not faced a public-health challenge like the coronavirus since 1918. America is the disease's epicenter: New York and New Jersey have recorded the largest number of deaths. The United States accounts for about a quarter of global

---

1 Boccia, Romina, and Justin Bogie. "This Is How Big the COVID-19 CARES Act Relief Bill Is." The Heritage Foundation, 20 Apr. 2020, https://www.heritage.org/budget-and-spending/commentary/how-big-the-covid-19-cares-act-relief-bill.

infections and more than one-fifth of global deaths. Economically, the U.S. has suffered damage that can scarcely be quantified—damage that has crossed the threshold of historical comparisons to the Great Depression, entering an uncharted realm. Even when normal life resumes, whenever that may be, the damage is likely to extend for years. Workplaces, restaurants, public transit, live events such as sports or music, schooling, travel, medical care—all of these areas, and more, will be transformed by the pandemic.

We will not go back to how things were. We will live in a post-Covid-19 era.

So all-encompassing has this experience been for so many Americans, and for citizens around the world, and so challenging, in terms of making the necessary adaptations to living differently, that it is easy to overlook the historical and political nature of what has occurred—and continues to occur. The historical nature is simple: our world will change, cities will change, economies will change, as a result of the virus, as they have in the past in response to other great plagues of contagious disease, from cholera to bubonic plague to influenza.

The global political ramifications, however, are more often overlooked. Most Americans, understandably, will focus their political judgments domestically—on the looming 2020 presidential campaign, and on whether, in their judgment, Donald Trump deserves another term in office; or whether Joe Biden and the Democrats, tireless critics of the administration's Covid-19 preparedness and ongoing response, should take the reins of national leadership. All of that will be adjudicated at the polls in November.

But there is a much bigger matter to be assessed, strange though it may sound to say so, in a presidential election year.

And that is the matter of China. It was China, after all, that foisted the coronavirus upon the world, first through its negligence and then through its coverup and suppression of information about Covid-19. The coronavirus added a whole new context to an ongoing trade war between China and the United States and to the two nations' struggle for supremacy in the South China Sea and, more generally, for global leadership—a struggle made ever-more daunting for the U.S. by rising Chinese adventurism, not only in the South China Sea but also in Hong Kong and North Korea. And this broader context makes the story of Covid-19 even more troubling—for the virus's impact on the world would almost certainly have been less severe had the Communist government in Beijing not behaved as it did.

The result of it all has almost certainly benefited the Chinese in terms of global influence. The result in America, by contrast, has been mounting polarization and division, distracting us from the need to enhance and strengthen our global alliances for everything from coordinating efforts to fight the virus to standing up for democratic values around the world.

Amid all of the carnage, human and economic, questions swirl about the nature of this crisis, about its ramifications, and about the future of U.S.-China relations and the international order. As important as it is to understand how this happened, and why, it is also vital, from an American perspective, to appreciate how the ordeal of Covid-19 has added yet another dimension to the ongoing, sustained undermining of American political and institutional stability.

The Origins—and the Coverup

From the beginning, suspicion swirled about the origins of the virus, always focusing on two main sources. The first was Wuhan's notorious "wet markets," where live animals circulate adjacent to food sold for human consumption. The wet markets have long been regarded as havens for infection, having been identified as the source of the 2003–2004 outbreak of SARS, another acute respiratory disease, this one caused by a different coronavirus strain. The second suspected source is the Wuhan Institute of Virology, which has long done research on animal-borne viruses, including bat-borne viruses, of the kind that caused Covid-19. Those who favored the lab theory split into two camps. Some felt that the coronavirus had escaped the lab, and that Chinese incompetence in containing the spread led to the outbreak—made worse by Chinese Communist suppression of information, punishing those (including doctors) who sought to get the word out and warn the public (both in China and beyond), and even denying that the virus could be transmitted to humans. Others argued that the virus itself was human-engineered as a bioweapon.

There is no question that the Chinese wet markets are infection breeding grounds: indeed, the experience of SARS, an illness far deadlier but thankfully much less widespread than Covid-19, proves this point. And China's wet markets have been sources of other awful illnesses over the past generation and more. The Chinese have long resisted reforming unsanitary practices that have sickened so many people around the world, long before the advent of Covid-19. So, surmising that Covid-19, too, was born from the wet markets made intuitive sense. Wuhan was a haven for wet markets.

However, evidence has steadily become available calling this explanation into question—and pointing to the Wuhan Institute of Virology as the source of the coronavirus. As early as January 2020, *The Lancet*, Britain's leading medical journal, was reporting that many of the early Covid-19 cases in Wuhan did not come from the wet markets, though many scientists continue to see the markets as the likelier explanation. The U.S. government is investigating, and statements from officials indicate that they see the lab explanation as plausible. The Trump administration was "asking the Chinese Communist Party to allow experts to get in to that virology lab so that we can determine precisely where this virus began," said Secretary of State Mike Pompeo. "It's not political. This is about science and epidemiology."[2]

Indeed, the U.S. government has grown increasingly confident that the virus originated in the Wuhan lab—but not, as some critics allege, as an attempted bioweapon. In most U.S. official circles, the bioweapon theory is dismissed. "If I could just be clear, there is nothing to that," said Air Force Brig. Gen. Paul Friedrichs, the Joint Staff Surgeon, in April. "I am not worried about this as a bioweapon."[3] Instead, the prevailing government view is that the virus was natural in origin, and that the Chinese were attempting to prove that their "efforts to identify

---

2 "Secretary Michael R. Pompeo With Maria Bartiromo." Mornings with Maria, Fox Business, 17 Apr. 2020, https://www.state.gov/secretary-michael-r-pompeo-with-maria-bartiromo-of-mornings-with-maria-on-fox-business-network-2/

3 Mitchell, Ellen. "Joint Chiefs Chairman Says Majority of Evidence Points to Coronavirus Being Created through Nature." The Hill, 14 Apr. 2020, https://thehill.com/policy/defense/492811-joint-chiefs-chairman-says-majority-of-evidence-points-to-coronavirus-being.

and combat viruses are equal or greater than those of the U.S.," according to Fox News.[4]

Still, even if the virus was not intended as a weapon, that does not eliminate other questions about its potential genesis in the lab. The secrecy of Chinese officials makes clear that they have something to hide. Their refusal to allow inspections of the lab suggests to many that the wet market explanation is a cover story.

However, the question of the virus's origin is also, in an important sense, merely a detail to a final verdict on China's culpability. For, whether the virus was manmade or natural, there is the undeniable record of how China handled the virus once it was out of the lab—suppressing and covering up information in an attempt to obscure the truth about Covid-19.

Deception, from the beginning

From the outset, Beijing did not tell the truth about the coronavirus. It misled about the virus's existence; about its prevalence in the population; about its virulence; about its transmissibility; about the timeline of events of the virus's appearance and discovery—about everything. Put simply, the regime implemented a crude but massive coverup of what was going on in Wuhan. Chinese officials silenced doctors and destroyed lab samples; shut down or suppressed social media commentators; and assured the world, through their collaboration with the World Health Organization, that there was nothing to worry about. And all the while, as China did this, it was buying massive

---

4   Baier, Bret, and Gregg Re. "Sources Believe Coronavirus Outbreak Originated in Wuhan Lab as Part of China's Efforts to Compete with US." Fox News, 15 Apr. 2020, https://www.foxnews.com/politics/coronavirus-wuhan-lab-china-compete-us-sources.

quantities of personal protective equipment (PPE) on the world market, the better to keep it for its own medical workers—thus creating the shortage of these same goods that would soon bedevil other countries, especially the United States, in dire need of securing their own supplies. The Chinese also refused to provide disease samples to doctors working on vaccines.

Any apologetics for Beijing's coverup can be dismissed after the release of the "Five Eyes" intelligence dossier on the matter in early May 2020. The research, compiled by the intelligence agencies of the United States, Great Britain, Canada, Australia, and New Zealand, finds strong grounds for concluding that China engineered a coverup of all facets of the coronavirus crisis, deliberately concealing or destroying information crucial for the global community to be able to plan a response. The Chinese Communists' actions represented, in the words of the Five Eyes report, "an assault on international transparency."[5]

The Chinese began censoring news near the end of 2019, eliminating news of the virus on social media and Internet search engines, removing search terms including "SARS variation," "Wuhan Seafood market" and "Wuhan Unknown Pneumonia." A few days later, the country's National Health Commission issued an order prohibiting all publication about the disease. Soon after, Wuhan's Municipal Health Commission stopped releasing daily case updates, and did not restart this practice for nearly two weeks. Peking University First Hospital respiratory specialist Wang Guanga announced that the virus

---

5   Shaw, Adam, et al. "Leaked 'Five Eyes' Dossier on Alleged Chinese Coronavirus Coverup Consistent with US Findings, Officials Say." *Fox News*, 2 May 2020, https://www.foxnews.com/politics/five-eyes-dossier-chinese-coronavirus-coverup-u-s-findings.

was "under control" and caused only a "mild condition," neglecting to mention that he himself had been infected. Professors' labs were shut down, and Beijing refused to share samples with a University of Texas lab.

Most egregiously, Chinese authorities denied that the virus could even be transmitted to humans until January 20, 2020. The World Health Organization disseminated this false information, until the Chinese corrected it.

The Chinese deliberately undercounted the number of cases, too. This was pointed out by Dr. Deborah Birx, the Trump administration's coronavirus Task Force coordinator, who, along with Dr. Anthony Fauci, became a household name and familiar face during the crisis in the United States. Dr. Birx is a diplomatic public-health professional, but her words contained a veiled condemnation of China: "I think when you looked at the China data originally, and you said, 'Oh, well there's 80 million people,' or 20 million people in Wuhan and 80 million people in Hubei, and they come up with a number of 50,000, you start thinking of this more like SARS than you do this kind of global pandemic," she said at a press briefing on March 31. "So I think the medical community made—interpreted the Chinese data as, that this was serious but smaller than anyone expected, because I think probably we were missing a significant amount of the data, now that when we see what happened to Italy and we see what happened to Spain."[6]

---

6 "Remarks by President Trump, Vice President Pence, and Members of the Coronavirus Task Force in Press Briefing," PRESIDENT TRUMP WITH CORONA-VIRUS TASK FORCE BRIEFING, C-SPAN, 31 Mar. 2020, https://www.c-span.org/video/?c4865568/user-clip-dr-brix-wishes-truth-china

We were missing a significant amount of data. A polite way to put it.

Were these errors the result of honest misunderstanding? No. Experts in Hong Kong and in Taiwan had been raising concerns about human transmission for weeks beforehand.

And all along, international travel continued, with the Chinese assuring their neighbors and other countries, like the United States, that there was no reason to restrict it. In fact, Beijing's urgings continued throughout February—though by then President Trump, in a move at first condemned but later adopted around the world, had shut down U.S. airline travel to China. And, of course, during this period international travel proceeded, with millions going into and out of China. Millions left Wuhan itself, taking flights from the afflicted Chinese city to cities around the world—until January 23, when Beijing locked the city down. It is no great mystery, then, that the virus spread globally.

United States intelligence officials are convinced that the Chinese knew about the contagiousness of the virus in December, and transcripts have revealed officials in the Communist Party discussing it in internal communications in January—reflecting their understanding of the dangers, even as they continued to mislead the world.

These deceptions have proved devastating. Until truth was brought to the matter, Western health officials did not understand the seriousness of the illness (especially to certain groups), its highly contagious nature, or the fact that, by listening to Chinese assurances and permitting travel to continue, they were unwittingly importing the virus into their countries at soon-to-be disabling levels. As late as early March, it was still not clear to major Western health officials how serious things were. Even the much-celebrated Dr. Fauci was assuring young-er Americans as late as early March that it was safe for them to travel on cruise ships.

WHO: a dupe, or a willing co-conspirator?

The failure of the World Health Organization throughout this matter cannot be overstated. The organization, nominal-ly charged with global health coordination and information, failed to protect the international community from what has become an epochal public-health and economic catastrophe. Some see WHO as China's dupe, for parroting Beijing's denial that the virus posed no danger of human transmission; others see the organization as an active co-conspirator of disinforma-tion. As with the debate about the origin of the virus itself, ei-ther conclusion is damning enough.

Though evidence suggests that Wuhan doctors knew by mid-December that human-to-human transmission was oc-curring, Beijing told WHO that this was not the case. On Janu-ary 14, the organization issued a tweet that would become no-torious: "Preliminary investigations conducted by the Chinese authorities have found no clear evidence of human-to-human transmission of the novel #coronavirus (2019-nCoV) identified in #Wuhan, #China."[7] The damage this did is incalculable.

The co-conspirator allegation, though scoffed at by deter-mined globalist supporters of the organization, seems increas-ingly plausible after a report in Germany's *Der Spiegel* claim-

---

7   Givas, Nick. "WHO Haunted by January Tweet Saying China Found No Human Transmission of Coronavirus." Fox News, 18 Mar. 2020, https://www.foxnews.com/world/world-health-organization-january-tweet-china-human-transmission-coronavirus.

ing that Chinese president Xi Jinping directly intervened with WHO on January 21, asking director-general Tedros Adhanom Ghebreyesus to delay making a public warning about human-to-human transmission of the virus and declaring a global pandemic. The allegations come from an investigation by Germany's Federal Intelligence Service, the BND, which "estimates that China's information policy lost four to six weeks to fight the virus worldwide."[8]

Gordon Chang, a withering critic of Beijing, also sees WHO as an active collaborator in the Chinese suppression of information. "It's very clear now that the Chinese Communist Party and the World Health Organization didn't put that information out into the international space as they're required to do in a timely fashion."[9] The actions were intentional, he concludes. It's hard to disagree, especially considering the close relationship between the WHO and Beijing; how Beijing played a leading role in Tedros's selection to head up the organization; and the fact that Tedros himself is a consummate practitioner of cronyism with Third World dictators, such as China, which he demonstrated when, stung by criticism of his performance, he complained about racist attacks—and blamed Taiwan for them.

_____

8 Court, Andrew, and Jack Elsom. "China's President Xi Jinping 'Personally Asked WHO to Hold Back Information about Human-to-Human Transmission and Delayed the Global Response by Four to Six WEEKS' at the Start of the COVID-19 Outbreak, Bombshell Report Claims." Daily Mail, 10 May 2020, https://www.dailymail.co.uk/news/article-8304471/Chinas-president-Xi-Jinping-personally-requested-delay-COVID-19-pandemic-warning.html.

9 Musto, Julia. "Gordon Chang: China and WHO Acted Maliciously, Tried to Deceive the World." Fox News, 18 Apr. 2020, https://www.foxnews.com/media/gordon-chang-china-world-health-organization-coronavirus-deceipt.

It's also important to recognize Tedros's role in the corona-virus crisis in a broader context: he represents the free rein that Beijing has to influence an organization of global reach, in the absence of any United States role. Beijing likely wouldn't have been able to install someone like Tedros if the Trump adminis-tration had shown any interest in the matter, or any recognition of WHO's importance globally. But beyond throwing lots of Washington dollars at WHO, the administration showed little interest in its existence. And in late May, Trump announced that the United States would terminate its relationship with WHO.

And amid all this, to add insult to injury, Beijing claimed credit for its performance on stopping the virus's spread in Chi-na; for keeping its caseloads remarkably low (though everyone knew that their numbers were doctored); and for helping the world prepare, even becoming a supplier to other nations of medical supplies, tests, and protective gear—much of which proved to be defective and unusable. It's a catalogue of revision-ism breathtaking in scope.

Deception Plus Propaganda

Beijing's manipulations did not stop with medical and pub-lic-health information. The Chinese also orchestrated an in-tense campaign of propaganda and deception, looking to con-fuse and divide public opinion in the West, especially in the United States. The most egregious of their efforts involve re-peated claims that the coronavirus was brought into China by the United States military. The claim was touted by Zhao Lijian, China's Ministry of Foreign Affairs spokesperson, who first cir-culated it in a tweet: "It might be US army who brought the epidemic to Wuhan. Be transparent! Make public your data! US owe us an explanation!"[10] Chinese embassies and consulates then echoed the accusations in their own tweets. The claims, patently absurd, have been repeated elsewhere, and, in the manner of conspiracy theories, have even gained some traction among respectable people.

Even those who rightly reject China's ludicrous claims about American responsibility for the virus have been vulnerable to other Chinese manipulations, sometimes without even knowing it. In March 2020, when dread began descending on the United States as the nation braced for a massive virus outbreak and prepared to begin self-quarantining, millions of Americans were bombarded with cellphone, social media, and computer messages warning of an imminent national lockdown initiated by the Trump administration. One of the messages claimed that the government would "announce this as soon as they have troops in place to help prevent looters and rioters," and cited a source in the Department of Homeland Security, who had supposedly said that "he got the call last night and was told to pack and be prepared for the call today with his dispatch orders."[11]

---

10 Zhao, Lijian (zlj517). "2/2 CDC was caught on the spot. When did patient zero begin in US? How many people are infected? What are the names of the hospitals? It might be US army who brought the epidemic to Wuhan. Be transparent! Make public your data! US owe us an explanation!" 12 March 2020, 10:37 AM. Tweet, https://twitter.com/zlj517/status/1238111898828066823?ref_src=twsrc%5Etf-w%7Ctwcamp%5Etweetembed%7Ctwterm%5E1238111898828066823&ref_url=https%3A%2F%2Fwww.nbcnews.com%2Fnews%2Fworld%2Fcoronavirus-chinese-official-suggests-u-s-army-blame-outbreak-n1157826

11 Wong, Edward, et al. "Chinese Agents Helped Spread Messages That Sowed Virus Panic in U.S., Officials Say." The New York Times, 23 Apr. 2020, https://www.nytimes.com/2020/04/22/us/politics/coronavirus-china-disinformation.html?action=-click&module=Top Stories&pgtype=Homepage.

The messages continued at such volume and intensity that the administration finally had to address them. The National Security Council issued a tweet declaring that all such messages were fakes.

Of course, the United States *did* essentially lock itself down, beginning in March, though this "lockdown," severe as it has been, was never ordered in the form of a federal emergency or declaration of martial law. It was implemented and managed at the state and local level. The Trump administration did call, in mid-March, for two weeks of social distancing and essential isolation, an instruction that was then repeatedly renewed afterward. Only in May did some states begin initiating their own partial re-openings. But the United States was never ordered to shut down by the federal government; President Trump consistently declared that state governors should decide for their own states.

Still, many readers will remember hearing such rumors in early March, when anxiety began spreading around the United States like a virus of its own. As it turns out, the broad dissemination of these messages—which were already circulating from other sources—was the work of Beijing, as United States intelligence officials have since determined. The officials were particularly struck by Chinese ability to push these messages to American cellphones, a capability they had not seen before, and accomplished, in part, by using encrypted messaging apps. Another striking aspect: the Chinese implementers used techniques more associated with Russian trolls, especially the creation of fake social media accounts. It's likely, too, that the messages were not spread merely by Chinese trolls or hackers, but also by Chinese spies at diplomatic missions here, a possibility that the U.S. is investigating further.

The tactics were effective for reasons particular to both so-cial media and to the specifics of the virus crisis. Social media "memes" are, by their nature, viral—and the Chinese knew that these messages, once in the hands of a sufficient number of American social media users, would be shared and spread wide-ly, as indeed they were. Second, because anxiety about the virus was already growing rapidly, and because institutional trust has broken down in the United States, amid deepening political po-larization, the climate was perfect for viral conspiracy theories and panic-inducing warnings to gain great traction—and they did. The tactic shows that Beijing wanted to deepen political divisions in the United States and spread fear and dissension.

In this goal, too, one sees a Russian influence.

Indeed, the Russian tie to what China did with the "lockdown" warnings represents a chilling reminder of how, even when Mos-cow and Beijing aren't working directly together, they are increas-ingly running operations from the same playbook. Those efforts are made even easier when, on one side, the political Right in America sees much of the lockdown efforts as authoritarianism run amok, even questioning whether individuals like Fauci can be trusted, and, in some cases, even echoing some conspiratorial theories about the virus's origins; and when the Left sees every-thing that the Trump administration does as destructive, whether it's too authoritarian or not authoritarian enough (the Left has often seemed unable to make up its mind, during the crisis, in this regard). And it's made worse, too, when the president him-self exhibits such erratic leadership, even dismissing such exter-nal efforts by America's leading adversary to demoralize our peo-ple. "They do it and we do it and we call them different things," Trump said of the Chinese messages. "Every country does it."

With that kind of nihilistic attitude—one that Trump has shown before, in seeming to echo critiques by authoritarian countries of American policies—China will not find it hard to expand its efforts to shape American public opinion. And, in Trump, Xi has found an adversary only intermittently serious. In the early days of the coronavirus crisis, Trump touted Xi's handling of the virus, and China's, with a tweet in which he exuded, "Much respect!" Not long afterward, he was talking about the "Chinese virus." By May, he was saying things like, "We could cut off the whole relationship."[12] Having an unpredictable, mercurial (some would say unstable) president has surely made America's battle against the virus even harder.

Still, whatever one wants to say about the Trump administration and its record on the coronavirus—it will surely lead all assessments of his presidency—it is a remarkable testament to the skill of Chinese propaganda and China's deep penetration into U.S. institutional life that American media have unleashed many more words lambasting the Trump administration's failures than they have calling out Beijing for causing the virus and inflicting it on the world.

It is also a remarkable testament to the depths of political polarization in the United States that the Democrats, the party out of power in the White House at the moment, are so consumed by their animus for Trump that they cannot seem to bring themselves to condemn China. "The reason that we're in the crisis that we are today is not because of anything China

12   Bartiromo, Maria. "Trump on China: 'We Could Cut off the Whole Relationship'." Fox Business, 14 May 2020, https://www.foxbusiness.com/politics/trump-on-china-we-could-cut-off-the-whole-relationship.

did," said Senator Chris Murphy of Connecticut, instead blaming Trump for his administration's slow response.[13] Others in the party have said similar things.

Trump's leadership during the crisis has unquestionably left much to be desired. Yet his failures do not change the fact that China has essentially declared a new cold war on the United States.

A New Cold War

It seems clear now that Covid-19 will take a place in world history, a seismic event of the twenty-first century whose effects will only be fully understood over many years, even decades. What also seems clear is that the United States-China relationship will change—indeed, must change. The question is how, and along what lines.

Among Americans, anger at China runs high. American voters may, in the short term, choose to blame the Trump administration at the polls in November 2020; in the long term, whomever they vote for, most Americans understand that China is responsible for a global catastrophe that could have been greatly minimized or even averted entirely had Beijing simply told the truth about it from the beginning. No number of missteps, from often-bungling Western governments, can disguise Beijing's fundamental culpability. Recent polls in the United States suggest that Americans understand this—overwhelm-

---

13 Hoonhout, Tobias. "Sen. Chris Murphy: 'The Reason We Are in This Crisis Today Is Not Because of Anything China Did.'" National Review, 15 Apr. 2020, https://www.nationalreview.com/news/sen-chris-murphy-the-reason-we-are-in-this-crisis-today-is-not-because-of-anything-china-did/.

ing majorities blame China for causing this disaster. Moreover, the coronavirus has darkened Americans' views of China more broadly. A Pew poll showed two-thirds of American respondents now view China negatively.[14]

American policymakers—regardless of whether they are part of a Trump or Joe Biden administration in 2021—will have to respond to the American people's darkening view of China. Even the most devout China apologists—and their numbers are legion in the federal government, in the private sector, and in the American media—will have to recognize that the coronavirus has ripped the curtain down on Beijing's masquerade as a responsible member of the global community. China's refusal to take responsibility for the virus has revealed the true character of the Communist regime even for those who had not been willing to acknowledge the obvious before. If U.S. officials, of either party, hope genuinely to serve the American national interest, then we're going to see changes in the years ahead.

Some of those changes are already afoot. The Trump administration has cut investment ties, for example, between U.S. federal retirement funds and Chinese equities. The move affects about $4 billion in assets.[15]

Meantime, U.S. lawmakers, in tandem with Canadian counterparts and Indian attorneys, are pursuing various legal ac-

---

14   Devlin, Kat, et al. "U.S. Views of China Increasingly Negative Amid Coronavirus Outbreak." Pew Research Center, 21 Apr. 2020, https://www.pewresearch.org/global /2020/04/21/u-s-views-of-china-increasingly-negative-amid-coronavirus-outbreak/.

15   Bartiromo, Maria. "Trump on China: 'We Could Cut off the Whole Relationship'." Fox Business, 14 May 2020, https://www.foxbusiness.com/politics/trump-on-china-we-could-cut-off-the-whole-relationship.

tions, including reparations, against China for inflicting the coronavirus on the world, causing hundreds of thousands of deaths and hundreds of billions, if not trillions, in economic damage. Republican Senator Marsha Blackburn of Tennessee has sponsored a Senate resolution calling on Beijing to forgive some of its holdings of American debt. Private American citizens have filed lawsuits against China seeking damages, including a $20 trillion class-action suit in Texas. Beijing will pay no heed to Blackburn's gesture, and the Foreign Sovereign Immunities Act will almost surely protect it against citizen claims, but these actions indicate the resentment against China felt by large portions of the American public.

Some China observers, such as Gordon Chang, argue that the United States should retaliate by seizing China's holdings of U.S. Treasury obligations—but only in tandem with our allies and issuers of other major currencies. "If we act alone," Chang argues, "China is going to say that we repudiated our debt. We're going to take a reputational hit, which is going to be a big one… they're going to say that we are an irresponsible member of the global financial system, and that the dollar shouldn't be the reserve currency of the world." But if the U.S. acts in concert with allies, then "we can take away that argument from China."[16]

The anger extends far beyond Washington's shores. India's bar association, in tandem with the International Council of Jurists (ICJ), is appealing to the United Nations Human Rights Council

---

16 "GORDON CHANG: SEIZE CHINA'S U.S. TREASURY HOLDINGS IN CONJUNCTION WITH ALLIES." Breitbart News Daily, SiriusXM Patriot 125, 10 Apr. 2020, https://americanpriority.com/news/gordon-chang-seize-chinas-u-s-treasury-holdings-in-conjunction-with-allies/

for compensation from China for "surreptitiously developing a biological weapon capable of mass destruction." The ICJ's president called Covid-19 a "crime against humanity," caused by China, which has "deliberately concealed crucial information about coronavirus." He asked the UN to "enquire and direct China and to adequately compensate international community and member states, particularly India, for surreptitiously developing a biological weapon capable of mass destruction of mankind."[17] He further alleged that China had exploited the virus with the intention of controlling the global economy and taking advantage of countries weakened by the virus and facing economic collapse.

Beijing's shameful actions in regard to medical equipment and supplies, as well as testing materials—buying up these materials on the global market, thus causing shortages, and then selling everything from defective equipment to bad tests to countries facing virus outbreaks—has caused anger and resentment in capitals around the world. Several countries in Asia and Europe, including Great Britain and Spain, have sent these useless materials back to Beijing.

And more recent steps in Washington reflect a broader awareness developing of the scope and range of the response needed.

In June, President Trump signed legislation imposing sanctions on the Chinese officials responsible for the forced labor camps that Beijing has set up for Uighur Muslims. Trump said that the new law "holds accountable perpetrators of human rights violations and abuses such as the systematic use of in-

---

17 "Global Body of Jurists Moves UNHRC to Seek Compensation from China." Tribune News Service India, 4 Apr. 2020, https://www.tribuneindia.com/news/nation/global-body-of-jurists-moves-unhrc-to-seek-compensation-from-china-65824.

doctrination camps, forced labor, and intrusive surveillance to eradicate the ethnic identity and religious beliefs of Uyghurs and other minorities in China."[18]

Another hopeful sign: in July, the House of Representatives passed a bill imposing sanctions on banks that do business with Chinese officials involved in Beijing's ongoing crackdown against the Hong Kong democracy movement—specifically, those officials who helped implement the new national security law, which is designed to suppress dissent. Further, in August, President Trump imposed the first US sanctions against officials from China and Hong Kong over suppression of pro-democracy protests and dissent in the territory, seeking to punish China for its repression in Hong Kong.

We should hope that these steps, which suggest a clear-eyed recognition of the Chinese regime's systematic and wide-ranging abuses, will mark a new focus and determination on the part of American policymakers—whether in the incumbent administration or a successor one—in dealing with Beijing. We should hope, that is, that such measures reflect a dawning recognition of what we need to do and why we need to do it—and not just in the short term, but as an adaptation of American foreign policy for the foreseeable future.

Raising the stakes further, our foreign policy as it relates to China must confront the threat they pose in other parts of the world, particularly the Middle East, where there are American intelligence reports in August that China is helping Saudi Ara-

---

18   Chalfant, Morgan. "Trump signs bill to sanction Chinese officials over Uighur rights," The Hill, 17 June 2020, https://thehill.com/policy/international/503245-trump-signs-bill-to-sanction-chinese-officials-over-uighur-rights.

bia build up its ability to produce and refine the nuclear fuel necessary to the development of nuclear weapons.[19]

The bottom line is this: the American relationship with China is about to change, just as the world's relationship with China is about to change. All the momentum must point to reduced dependency on China, and to a more realistic definition of our relationship with Beijing. Going forward, the U.S. must seek a workable but toughminded relationship, one that recognizes China as an explicit adversary, yet one too large and consequential in the world today to avoid dealings with altogether. We must reject both an unrealistic "decoupling" and the gullible, uncritical, and self-dealing relationship that American elites fostered with China over the last several decades. Politically, economically, militarily, the United States is challenged today to define its approach to China—a more formidable nation-state adversary than any we have faced since the Cold War with the Soviet Union. We face a new Cold War.

But not just with China.

The new Cold War is also with the former Soviet Union—with Vladimir Putin's Russia. That's a sobering reality that the pandemic has tended to obscure, though even amid the on-going struggle against Covid-19, the Russian presence can be seen. In June 2020, for example, came the stunning news that Russian operatives had offered "bounties" to Taliban militants to kill American troops in Afghanistan. It appears that at least

---

19   Mazzetti, Mark, David E. Sanger and William J. Broad. "U.S. Examines Whether Saudi Nuclear Program Could Lead to Bomb Effort." New York Times, 5 August 2020, https://www.nytimes.com/2020/08/05/us/politics/us-examines-saudi-nuclear-program.html

some of these attacks did result in American deaths.[20] The news dramatized again how willingly Putin's Russia violates norms of international relations to achieve its goals, and it was all made worse by President Trump's appalling refusal to acknowledge the veracity of the reports, much less take any retaliatory action. The Taliban bounty story served as another harrowing reminder that the United States has more than one determined authoritarian adversary on the global stage—and no reliable leadership, at present, with which to confront them.

Further, as David Sanger and Eric Schmitt reported in the New York Times, "it doesn't require a top-secret clearance and access to the government's most classified information" to understand that the alleged bounties to the Taliban were only one facet of Russian aggression against the United States in the first half of 2020.[21] Indeed, Americans working from home have experienced cyberattacks against their private US companies' computer systems, Russian internet trolls continue to exploit American voters on social media, and Russian jets have been testing US and allies' air defenses from the Mediterranean Sea to the Alaskan coast. Without question, these latest aggressions, particularly in the era of COVID-19, represent some of the

---

20   Nakashima, Ellen, DeYoung, Karen, Ryan, Missy, and Hudson, John. "Russian bounties to Taliban-linked militants resulted in deaths of U.S. troops, according to intelligence assessments." Washington Post, 28 June 2020, https://www.washingtonpost.com/national-security/russian-bounties-to-taliban-linked-militants-resulted-in-deaths-of-us-troops-according-to-intelligence-assessments/2020/06/28/74ffaec2-b96a-11ea-80b9-40ece9a701dc_story.html

21   Sanger, David, and Eric Schmitt. "Trump's New Russia Problem: Unread Intelligence and Missing Strategy." New York Times, 1 July 2020, https://www.nytimes.com/2020/07/01/us/politics/trump-putin-russia-taliban-bounty.html

most brazen actions directly against the United States since I first began analyzing Putin's authoritarian ascendency in-depth in my 2014 book, *The Russia-China Axis: The New Cold War and America's Crisis of Leadership.* And these are to say nothing of other Russian incursions, these into nations where America once held strong influence, such as Syria and Venezuela, which have occurred without any real American response, much less pushback.

Before the coronavirus crisis, I had written about the twin challenge that these two nations posed to the United States and to Western democracies, especially as they deepened a strategic, military, and economic partnership—becoming, as I called them in a previous book, a "new Axis." I was engaged in writing this new book, which I intended both as a summary of how closely my warnings have been borne out by events over the past decade and as a warning of what's to come, when Covid-19 broke out.

Covid-19 and the reconfigured world only make the message of this book more pressing and urgent—and my past warnings more prescient, if I may say so. Few would dispute now that the United States faces grim challenges ahead, in everything from economic recovery to economic reorganization—we need to get back our pharmaceutical manufacturing capacity, for example—to our military posture to our capabilities in cyber-intelligence.

During the worst of the infection period, some were heard to say that viruses don't play favorites: they strike down the wealthy and the poor, the prominent and the anonymous, in this country or in that one. Indeed: illness and disease have always had a kind of ruthless honesty. They afflict wherever they can. It is this same kind of ruthless honesty that the United

States now needs to apply to itself and its relations with China—and with China's partner, Russia.

The coronavirus blew up an unsustainable world order. The damage it has done should not be minimized or denied. But it may yet prove a grim blessing, if it serves, at last, as a wake-up call to the United States—a deadly but valuable reminder of truths both timeless and specific.

The timeless truth: the world is ever dangerous, and no great nation has ever existed that did not face persistent opposition from mortal foes.

The specific truth: those mortal foes, today, are in Beijing and in Moscow.

The virus can be cured with a vaccine when one is available. Decades of American self-destructiveness and self-delusion can be cured, too—but only by a painful recognition of the daunting realities we face and a determined resolve to address them.

CHAPTER ONE

Russia, China, and the American Retreat

I N 2014, I PUBLISHED (WITH MELIK KAYLAN) A BOOK ENTI-tled *The Russia-China Axis: The New Cold War and America's Crisis of Leadership.* Since then, I have published two addition-al books focusing on Vladimir Putin's aggression and strategic plans to undermine the international order and the Western democratic alliance. But as alarming as Putin's actions have been, it is his deepening relationship with Chinese president Xi Jinping that presents the most daunting challenge of all.

Our warnings in *The Russia-China Axis* were not only pre-scient—they remain even more relevant to the situation today than they were then:

> Russia and China now cooperate and coordinate to an unprecedented degree—politically, militarily, eco-nomically—and their cooperation, almost without deviation, carries anti-U.S. and anti-Western ramifi-cations. Russia, China, and a constellation of satellite states seek to undermine American power, dislodge

America from its leading position in the world, and establish a new, anti-Western global power structure… In short, there is a new Cold War in progress, with our old adversaries back in the game, more powerful than they have been for decades… The stakes are enormous. If we don't build awareness of what China and Russia are up to, greatly improve our understanding of their actions and motives, and take steps to defend ourselves and our interests, we will see our economic and political well-being threatened. And we'll watch as the international order tilts toward authoritarianism and away from democratic ideals and freedoms.

That would be a tragedy for America and for the world.

The tragedy has been unfolding before us for years now—long before Covid-19 arrived and scrambled global realities. For years before the coronavirus, the specter of the Russia-China axis hovered over the American, and Western, future. And years before the coronavirus, it stopped being merely a dark prospect but had instead become an accelerating reality. And yet, even with all the damage now accruing that reality is one that the United States seems to lack the insight to understand and the will to resist.

In the years since *The Russia-China Axis* was published, the problem has metastasized into an existential one for America and the West. Both Russia and China are authoritarian countries that explicitly reject the Western/American vision of liberty and democracy, and they have been steadily on the march in recent years to carve out an alternative world order. Consider, for example, Russian expansionism and aggression in Ukraine, Chinese expansionism in Africa, or both regimes' assistance to and support for rogue regimes, from Pyongyang to Tehran—carried out often with the acquiescence or indifference of U.S. presidential administrations.

The advance of China has proceeded across a generation of American presidential administrations. In U.S. official circles, a persistent refrain dominated and guided policymaking: integrating China into the international system and finding grounds for commonality was more important than standing up to Beijing on its human-rights abuses, free-trade violations, neo-colonialist behavior, and enabling of North Korean nuclear blackmail. To his credit, President Donald Trump has at least rhetorically challenged that model, sometimes dramatically, as when he has publicly called out China for its trade practices. Substantively, Trump has even initiated a trade war with Beijing—and in the wake of the virus, a host of new, tougher policy responses is possible, though Americans should not assume that anything is guaranteed.

Why not? Because the hold of China on U.S. policymaking, both economic and otherwise, remains very strong. In innumerable ways, the Trump administration has not challenged China; has in fact maintained a status quo, and certainly it has done so in regards to its brutal suppressions of human rights, whether domestically or, more recently, in Hong Kong. And it does, as did previous administrations, because the perceived cost of alienating Beijing, or losing various trade inflows, and of possibly risking military confrontation in the Pacific, are all regarded as too high a price to pay. A tougher China policy is surely needed; indeed, a whole rethinking of our China relationship is overdue. But up to now, there is little evidence that such things are taking shape, beyond small measures and symbolic gestures. Let us hope that bigger steps are in store.

Russia's advances have come despite different approaches taken by various U.S. administrations. After the end of the Cold War, Bill Clinton planted the seeds for a rebirth of Russian nationalism by welcoming former Soviet satellites into NATO. George W. Bush continued that effort, naïve to how American triumphalism was alienating Putin, whom he continued to view as an ally until near the end of this presidency. Barack Obama combined the worst of both worlds, slapping economic sanctions on Moscow and condemning its behavior internationally while doing nothing tangible to stop it—thus closing doors to Putin diplomatically while emboldening him politically and strategically. Finally, Donald Trump has exhibited a highly erratic approach: his administration's substantive policies have been tougher than his predecessors, yet his rhetorical apologia for Putin, up to and including Russian spying and sabotage of American elections, has broken every model of American diplomatic utterance. More substantively, Trump's indifference to the cause of the Ukrainian freedom fighters—as demonstrated in his infamous quid pro quo, which led to his impeachment—as well as his abandonment of the Middle East to Putin in Syria, have made his administration, on balance, the most pro-Russia in memory.

Needless to say, this long record of American policymaking toward Russia and China has been a dismal failure. The United States must wake up—starting in Washington—if it is going to take on the challenge posed by the Russia/China axis.

Closer and Closer

How close are Russia and China—and does their relationship qualify as an alliance, in name or deed? Listen to the words the countries use themselves: "China and Russia are together now like lips and teeth," says Li Hui, China's ambassador to Russia. Xi Jinping has visited Moscow more than any other global capital since he became Chinese premier. He and Putin have met more than two dozen times. Xi has called Putin "my best, most intimate friend," and given him China's friendship medal. In Moscow, the Foreign Ministry describes the China relationship as a "comprehensive, equal, and trust-based partnership and strategic cooperation."[22]

I've been warning about the threat of the deepening Russia-China axis for nearly a decade, and I'm heartened by how many mainstream thinkers have now begun to come around to the dangers. In January 2019, the U.S. intelligence community released its annual Worldwide Threat Assessment. On its opening page, the report's authors made clear what challenge to American interests was now top of mind:

> Threats to U.S. national security will expand and diversify in the coming year, driven in part by China and Russia as they respectively compete more intensely with the United States and its traditional allies and partners. This competition cuts across all domains, involves a race for technological and military superiority, and is increasingly about values. Russia and China seek to shape the international system and regional security dynamics and exert influence over the politics and economies of states in all regions of the world and especially in their respective backyards.

Russia and China, the authors maintained, "are more aligned than at any point since the mid-1950s."[1] This assessment re-

---

22 Allison, Graham. "China and Russia: A Strategic Alliance in the Making." National Interest, 14 Dec. 2020, https://nationalinterest.org/feature/china-and-russia-strategic-alliance-making-38727.

flects, at long last, a recognition on the part of U.S. officials that Russia and China have become the dominant threat to American national security and national interests, and, perhaps most broadly, to the future of the democratic values and systems with which America is identified around the world.

Other experienced observers are also coming around to these views. "It is long since time that analysts and policymakers acknowledged the reality that is evolving right before their eyes and stopped taking refuge in clichés and wishful thinking," writes Stephen Blank, a senior fellow with the American Foreign Policy Council.[23] Along with Blank and others, I have long argued that observers need to look beneath appearances and see what is really going on. Just because Beijing and Moscow don't use the formal word "alliance" doesn't mean that they aren't functioning as an alliance. They have used every other conceivable term.

As Putin himself said in 2016 about the Moscow-Beijing relationship, "As we had never reached this level of relations before, our experts have had trouble defining today's general state of our common affairs. It turns out that to say we have strategic cooperation is not enough anymore. This is why we have started talking about a comprehensive partnership and strategic collaboration."[24]

What matters, of course, is not the terminology Beijing and Moscow use, but what, together, they are doing—and it's a lot.

---

23   Blank, Stephen. "Russia, China and Collaborative Actions: An Alliance in the Making." Second Line of Defense, 19 Jan. 2019, https://sldinfo.com/2019/01/russia-china-and-collaborative-actions-an-alliance-in-the-making/.

24   Blank, Stephen. "U.S. China Economic and Security Review Commission Testimony: The Russo-Chinese Alliance: What Are Its Limits?" American Foreign Policy Council, 28 Mar. 2019, https://www.afpc.org/publications/articles/congressional-testimony-the-russo-chinese-alliance-what-are-its-limits#_edn21.

Consider the most visible area: military cooperation.

In August 2018, Russia conducted its largest military exercise since the Cold War. *Vostok*, or East, an operation involving 300,000 Russian soldiers and 1,000 aircraft, took place in a military district of Russia that shares a border with China and North Korea. The most striking thing about the exercise, besides its size: the presence, for the first time, of Chinese troops. More than 3,000 Chinese soldiers took part.

"There is nothing on paper, but they are building a de facto military alliance," said a Moscow-based China analyst, about the two countries, and it seems foolhardy, at this point, to deny this reality.[25] Russia and China have held 30 major joint military exercises since 2003. These include joint naval exercises in the Mediterranean Sea in 2015, the South China Sea in 2016, and the Baltic Sea in 2017.

Then there are the Russia-China joint air and missile-defense exercises, held in 2017, and which, as Blank points out, required both nations to "put their cards on the table" and reveal their four "c's"—command, control, communications, and computer, along with intelligence and surveillance capabilities. That's a lot of sharing for two secretive countries, especially two with such a long history of animosity and distrust.

Cooperation has grown so much between the two nations that Russia isn't even blinking—at least, not publicly—at Chinese incursions into Central Asia, traditionally Moscow's sphere of influence, especially via its massive Belt and Road ini-

---

25   Grove, Thomas. "Russian Troops Gear Up for Massive War Games With Chinese Military." Wall Street Journal, 28 Aug. 2018, https://www.wsj.com/articles/russian-troops-gear-up-for-massive-war-games-with-chinese-military-1535466282.

tiative. Who would have ever thought that we would hear Putin say: "The main struggle, which is now underway, is that for global leadership and we are not going to contest China on this."[26] In fact, Russia even looks to benefit economically from the arrangement.

In its 2019 Worldwide Threat Assessment, U.S. intelligence also warned that the two countries were engaged in a "race for technological and military superiority."[27] It's gratifying that American intelligence is facing up to this fact, though the recognition comes not a moment too soon. While I have no interest in saying "I told you so," the many years lost in acknowledging these facts have cost the United States dearly.

It's going to cost the international community, too, because the two countries now march in near lockstep at the United Nations and in other multilateral environments. Moscow and Beijing are the world's leading advocates for multipolarity, in which power is balanced between competing global centers, and not centralized within one great power. The implicit critique, of course, is of the United States as the global superpower—the lone superpower, as it was, in the years after the Cold War ended. At the UN Security Council, Moscow and Beijing almost always vote—and veto—together, generally in opposi-

---

26   Allison, Graham. "China and Russia: A Strategic Alliance in the Making." National Interest, 14 Dec. 2020, https://nationalinterest.org/feature/china-and-russia-strategic-alliance-making-38727.

27   Coats, Daniel R. "WORLDWIDE THREAT ASSESSMENT OF THE US INTELLIGENCE COMMUNITY." Senate Select Committee on Intelligence, 29 Jan. 2019, https://www.intelligence.senate.gov/sites/default/files/documents/os-dcoats-012919.pdf?mod=article_inline&utm_source=newsletter&utm_medium=email&utm_campaign=newsletter_axiosam&stream=top.

tion to the United States' wishes. On North Korea and Iran, on Syria, on Libya, on Iraq, and on and on, the two countries share essentially congruent viewpoints.

"We feel—and our Chinese friends share this view—that our cooperation and coordination in the international arena are one of the most important stabilizing factors in the world system," said Russian Foreign Minister Sergei Lavrov in 2015. "We regularly coordinate our approaches to various conflicts, whether it is in the Middle East, North Africa or the Korean Peninsula. We have regular and frank and confidential consultations."[28] Bruno Maçães of the Hudson Institute writes: "The thing to remember is that both countries are obsessed with overturning the American-led global order."[29]

Indeed, Moscow and Beijing could not agree more that the main security threat to their future is the United States, which both see as a hegemonic power trying not only to impinge on their spheres of influence but also to undermine—even overthrow—their authoritarian regimes and impose democracy.

Economically, too, Moscow and Beijing are moving ever closer. Not only is Moscow hoping to benefit from China's economic penetration of Central Asia: it is also pivoting eastward in its economic orientation, and away from the West. China is already Russia's top trading partner, supplanting the U.S. and

---

28   Blank, Stephen. "Russia, China and Collaborative Actions: An Alliance in the Making." Second Line of Defense, 19 Jan. 2019, https://sldinfo.com/2019/01/russia-china-and-collaborative-actions-an-alliance-in-the-making/.

29   Maçães, Bruno. "Russia to China: Together We Can Rule the World." Hudson Institute, 19 Feb. 2019, https://www.hudson.org/research/14822-russia-to-china-together-we-can-rule-the-world.

Germany. And, reciprocally, Russia is the top supplier of crude oil to China. Russian gas has huge market opportunities in China, which will soon become Moscow's Number Two gas market, after the completion of the Power of Siberia pipeline in 2019. The overall trade relationship between the two countries continues to grow, exceeding $100 billion for the first time in 2018. And the two countries are beginning to increase the amount of trade they do with one another in their own national currencies.

In short, this is a relationship that deserves to be called an alliance in all but name. As Richard Sakwa, Professor of Russian and European politics, puts it of the Russian-Chinese relationship: "It's an *alignment* [my emphasis] in which Russia and China will not do each other any harm. They will support each other when it's in their interests—and it's a game changer."[30]

I'm reminded of something that Zbigniew Brzezinski wrote in 2017, before he died. He warned of a "a grand coalition of China and Russia… united not by ideology but by complementary grievances." This coalition, he went on, "would be reminiscent in scale and scope of the challenge once posed by the Sino-Soviet bloc, though this time China would likely be the leader and Russia the follower." Brzezinski considered this Russia-China alliance "the most dangerous" global scenario.[31]

---

30   Peries, Sharmini. "Russia-China Alignment Challenges U.S. Hegemony." The Real News Network, https://therealnews.com/stories/russia-china-alignment-challenges-u-s-hegemony.

31   Allison, Graham. "China and Russia: A Strategic Alliance in the Making." National Interest, 14 Dec. 2020, https://nationalinterest.org/feature/china-and-russia-strategic-alliance-making-38727.

We seem to have arrived at the scenario that Brzezinski feared. Two crucial obstacles stand in the way of America addressing and combating the threat. The first is understanding it better. As I've noted above, it is only recently that American intelligence officials, policymakers, and media commentators have begun to get a true sense of what we face here. The second obstacle is a deeper and more difficult one: it is the retreat of American leadership around the world, the increasing abandonment of the American ideal overseas, of the idea that the United States has a vision that is worth fighting for, not just at home but abroad. Without some reclamation of that ideal, we cannot hope to prevail.

What We Face

America under Donald Trump is a long way off from the vision that John F. Kennedy spelled out in his Inaugural Speech on January 20, 1961—nearly 60 years ago. Kennedy's words that day remain famous, known to millions of Americans: "Let every nation know, whether it wishes us well or ill, that we shall pay any price, bear any burden, meet any hardship, support any friend, oppose any foe, in order to assure the survival and the success of liberty." Near the end of this great American speech, many remember that JFK said, "ask not what your country can do for you—ask what you can do for your country." Fewer people recall the sentence that immediately followed: "*My fellow citizens of the world: ask not what America will do for you, but what together we can do for the freedom of man.*" In that sentence, Kennedy broadened out the idea of doing for America to doing for the world—broadening out the American idea itself, an idea involving liberty and the rights of man, as an idea that was a birthright of the human race, not just of those fortunate few who call themselves Americans.

In my view, the history of the last century demonstrates that there is no substitute for this kind of American global leadership—missteps and all. Only the West, led by America, has achieved the kind of individual freedom and multicultural tolerance that the rest of the world sorely lacks. This democratic, tolerant, secular, and progress-oriented vision underpins the broader American idea as well: a free, open, and secular society, governed by the rule of law, in which individuals can advance as far as their abilities take them.

In our own time, it is fashionable to say that we don't want to foist our values upon others, because, after all, how can we say we're any better? And yet, the evidence is clear that the American idea *is* better—even if it often fumbles in practice. I happen to agree with, of all people, the Irish rock singer Bono, who said in 2016 that America was "the best idea the world ever came up with." He's right, and in his own, more contemporary way, he was echoing Kennedy's 1961 words.

Not so long ago, it appeared as if this view of America— and of democracy and human rights—was ascendant around the world. In 1993, Francis Fukuyama published an epochal book, *The End of History*, arguing that Western-style democracy had prevailed in the battle of ideological systems as the most self-evidently just system that man had yet devised—which did not mean, he hastened to add, that all societies would go on to choose such systems, or that the Western system's evident rectitude would protect it from threats or challenges. What he did believe, though, was that Western-style liberal democracy had won the intellectual argument between systems.

Yet, less than 30 years later, anti-democratic and outright authoritarian models of governance are in the ascendancy around the world, while the United States and its Western allies seem to have lost faith in their own ideals—while losing ground, not coincidentally, to these hostile forces around the world. Long before the coronavirus, advanced democracies, whether in the United States or Great Britain or France, faced ever-increasing political polarization and economic instability, while authoritarian nations—especially Russia and China—showed confidence and conviction in their political models and in their vision of a proper society and an orderly world. Thus, I thought it was fitting to give this book its dark title: *The End of Democracy?*

As a patriotic American, I have never been more concerned about our nation's future than now. Our politics are sclerotic and dysfunctional; our cultural cohesion is a thing of the past; our institutions have lost public legitimacy across the board; and our very identity as Americans seems increasingly to be subordinate to our tribal or ideological identities. All these things concern me greatly but overhanging them all is a loss of confidence in democratic ideals, both in America and around the world, and the concomitant rise of authoritarianism as a viable model of governance in the eyes of millions. At the center of that story are two nations—Russia and China—that together stand as a profound and fundamental challenge to the American and Western future, and to the future of democracy and human rights around the globe.

Is my title, *The End of Democracy*, an overstatement? In a literal sense, yes—we haven't lost democracy yet. But I sincerely believe that if we continue along the road we've been on, we may very well find ourselves living in systems we no longer recognize. Already, concessions have been made that we could never have imagined. Already, the losses are mounting.

America *must* lead—and its leadership depends not only on the revival of its institutions and the faith and confidence of its people but also on an approach and a vision that, put into practice, will deliver constructive results for the country, its allies, and the world at large. That means embracing a broad internationalist vision that Kennedy articulated, but one that, tragically, the United States under Donald Trump seems determined to jettison. I believe that, while Trump's confrontation with China is well-founded, his broader, anti-internationalist approach—one that antagonizes even American allies—will yield tragic results for America and the world, if pursued beyond his presidency.

Do we have the will to push back and reclaim the democracy that Jack Kennedy and the men of his generation fought a war to save? If so, our efforts must start with a better understanding of our determined adversaries in Moscow and Beijing, of how they have gathered so much momentum and power over recent years—and of how their successes have emboldened authoritarians and the cause of authoritarianism around the world, to the detriment of free societies and free people.

CHAPTER TWO

A New Dark Age:
Authoritarianism on the Rise

REMEMBER THE GREAT NEOLIBERAL MOMENT, AFTER THE convulsions of 1989—with the Berlin Wall no more, and the Iron Curtain down in Eastern Europe, and the Soviet Union about to dissolve? It was a heady and historic time, and the 1990s continued its momentum. Most observers assumed that the steady, upward march toward freedom would continue, and that the peoples of the world previously subjected to authoritarian dominance and cruelty would soon see liberation. And such a future was most dramatically envisioned for the two Communist countries that symbolized the Cold War showdown against the United States and its Western allies: The Soviet Union, soon to be known as Russia again, and no longer Communist; and the People's Republic of China.

Crucial to this move forward was an opening of markets to these countries, through the increasing expansion of global free trade agreements. After 1991, with Russia's Communist political system gone, Western optimists saw one piece of the puzzle already in place—Russia would adopt Western-style democratic governance. China wasn't there, yet—might not be for some time—but in either case, both countries, by embracing the Western free trade message, would liberalize their political cultures, even as they provided higher standards of living and greater economic opportunity for their beleaguered people. The free exchange of ideas and information—soon symbolized by the explosive growth of the Internet—the need for greater educational attainment in a competitive global marketplace, the rapid growth of technological expertise and expansion of investment, and the growing political expression of ordinary people would all move liberalization and freedom forward.

Western leaders certainly believed it. Against the new developments—especially the open Internet—authoritarianism stood little chance. If China tried to control the web, President Bill Clinton said in 2000, it would be "like trying to nail Jell-O to the wall." It couldn't be done; the web was a technological force of unswervingly democratic character. British Prime Minister Tony Blair was another apostle of global optimism. In 2005, he told reporters, after a meeting with Wen Jiabao, the Chinese premier: "The whole basis of the discussion I have had in a country that is developing very fast—where 100 million people now use the internet, and which is going to be the second-largest economy in the world—is that there is an unstoppable momentum toward greater political freedom." Capitalism and free trade went hand in hand with democracy.

What the optimists didn't realize is that Russian and Chinese leaders never saw things this way. All along, they viewed Western-style—especially American-style—democracy as a threat to their power and as a destabilizing force in their societies. True, they embraced the opportunities that the new global economy provided, but their confidence that trade and technology could be put to authoritarian uses has not only proved well-founded; it has also made sophisticated Western optimists look terribly naïve. Even the vaunted Internet, supposedly immune to authoritarian machinations, has become a pliable—and highly effective—tool of authoritarian control.

Far from liberalizing itself, China has developed and extended an all-powerful one-party state, with a massive state police that imprisons dissidents, censors expression, and conducts population surveillance on an ever-more massive and sophisticated scale. What Human Rights Watch calls the Great Firewall censors the Internet, and the Web in China now runs with multiple implanted apps and platforms that monitor usage, and, along with applications of artificial intelligence, conduct surveillance. Currently, the system is most aggressively used in Xinjiang, where it conducts exhaustive surveillance of the Uighur population, but plans are in place to extend it around the country.

Russia, too, has moved to strengthen its long tradition of authoritarian governance. After its brief dalliance with what might be called proto-democracy in the 1990s, Moscow has moved steadily away from democratic governance—and, in nearly 20 years of uninterrupted leadership under Vladimir Putin, Russia has become perhaps the global standard-bearer for nationalist, authoritarian, anti-democratic leadership. And Russia, too, has harnessed technology and surveillance to perpetuate and strengthen its political system of popular control. It, too, monitors Internet usage and collects and stores all activity. And as Americans know firsthand, Russian misinformation is highly effective at controlling and shaping public opinion.

As for free trade and capitalism, both countries have put it to their own uses. The Chinese Communists practice an aggressive, unabashed form of state-controlled capitalism, using the nation's powerful corporations as instruments of state control—and, increasingly, to shape opinions abroad, as well, especially among customers who don't wish to run afoul of Beijing by voicing unpopular opinions. This power reaches into the United States as well—as even NBA fans discovered, when a team general manager expressed support for the 2019 Hong Kong protests and the league office described his comments as "regrettable."[32] Superstar player LeBron James went further, suggesting that the general manager "wasn't educated" on China's role in Hong Kong when he made his comments.[33] Rather than a market-oriented instrument for greater economic openness, both countries use capitalism as an instrument of control and coercion.

What we're seeing is the most dramatic challenge to the Western democracies since the end of the Cold War.

What we're seeing is one of the most humbling lessons that history teaches: that no victory is permanent or assured—in this case, an inspiring victory over totalitarianism that seemed to auger a new future of liberation and human freedom.

What we're seeing is authoritarians using the technological and economic tools of the modern era to thwart indi-

32 "Rockets' General Manager's Hong Kong Comments Anger China." Associated Press, 7 Oct. 2019, https://apnews.com/0a660e9e10664e31bf6ee359c22058cf.

33 Togoh, Isabel. "LeBron James: Daryl Morey Was 'Misinformed' In NBA-China Dispute." Forbes, 15 Oct. 2019, https://www.forbes.com/sites/isabeltogoh/2019/10/15/lebron-james-daryl-morey-was-misinformed-in-nba-china-dispute/#61a4374f385c.

vidual freedom, crush democracy, and discredit the idea of self-government.

We've entered a new and troubling era in which authoritarianism is on the rise—and Russia and China are its lodestars, its guideposts, its power centers.

The Russian Shadow and the China Dream

Over nearly 20 years at the helm of Russian leadership, whether as president or prime minister, Vladimir Putin has steadily restricted civil liberties and free speech while imposing harsher domestic media control and deepening the militarism of Russian society. He has jailed—and, some say, arranged the murder of—dissidents and sent his security forces to crack down on political demonstrations. In fact, Putin's war on the free press has been described by close observers at home as worse than what the old Soviet Union did—even "Stalinist."[34]

Putin has elevated nationalism on the world stage, becoming the lead figure in its revival as a philosophy, but he does not merely pursue Russian self-interest—his efforts are also part of a concerted, counter-Western philosophy, one that rejects the core premises of open democratic societies, pluralism, and international norms. I have written extensively about this. Putin is not merely an adversary of the United States due to competing global interests; he is an adversary because he views the United States' democratic model as a threat to what he holds dear— Russian hegemony over its "near abroad," traditional Russian

---

34 Kendall, Bridget. "Russian propaganda machine 'worse than Soviet Union,'" *BBC News*, June 6, 2014, http://www.bbc.com/news/magazine-27713847.

culture, and an authoritarian political system not subject to the sometimes-destabilizing influence of democracy.

The Putin model of governance is bluntly and unapologetically authoritarian. Putin has instituted severe crackdowns on domestic democratic institutions within Russia: arresting protestors, purging the "liberal elite," censoring magazines and the Internet.[35] In 2016, top editors of RBC media group, an outlet that had infuriated Putin with some of its published stories, were forced to leave their posts for political reasons.[36] Editors of 12 other Russian media outlets were ousted as a result of government pressure over the past five years.[37] In 2014, Dozhd, described as Russia's one truly independent TV station, was nearly forced to halt operations. The reason was a law banning advertising on private cable and satellite channels. In collaboration with the Russian Orthodox Church, Putin's regime has also made life increasingly difficult for adherents of other religions.

American readers might assume that such brutish moves would ensure Putin's demise at the hands of Russian voters— at least, in a fair election—but they would be wrong. Up until recently, Putin's strong-man tactics have boosted his popularity. At present, surveys show much lower approval ratings amid

35 "Repression ahead," The Economist, June 1, 2013, http://www.economist.com/news/europe/21578716-vladimir-putins-crackdown-opponents-protesters-and-activist-groups-may-be-sign-fragility.

36 Trudolyubov, Maxim. "PUTIN'S ASSAULT ON RUSSIA'S FREE PRESS CONTINUES APACE," Newsweek, May 20, 2016, http://www.newsweek.com/putin-assault-russia-free-press-continues-apace-461571.

37 Arutunyan, Anna. "Russia crackdown on anti-Putin media worsens," USA Today, May 20, 2016, http://www.usatoday.com/story/news/world/2016/05/20/russia-crackdown-anti-putin-media-worsens/84583080/.

collapsing oil prices, the Covid-19 pandemic, and rising signs of discontent, but Putin has weathered similar storms before and come out stronger. And he has recently won court approval for an amendment that would allow him to run for president again after his current term ends in 2024. The change, though subject to a national referendum that has been postponed for the time being due to the coronavirus, could lead to Putin holding power in until 2036—and would make him Russia's longest-serving modern leader.[38]

Some argue that Putin's longstanding support demonstrates general Russian approval for an authoritative strongman leader, rather than affinity for Putin himself. "Eighty-two percent of Russians support the myth or the revival of the Great Russia status," says Lev Gudkov, director of Levada polling center, "as Putin makes people feel proud of Russia's greatness since the fall of the USSR."[39] Others have argued that what Russians truly yearn for is a return of the czars. Yet Putin's rule has been so distinctive, so clearly the product of a unique political personality and intelligence, that dismissing his broad national appeal as czarist nostalgia seems ill-considered.

Perhaps even more disturbing than Putin's popularity at home is his not-inconsiderable appeal to Westerners, including in the United States. In December 2016, 37% of Republicans in

---

38   Kantchev, Georgi. "Russia's Top Court Approves Plan Allowing Putin to Stay in Power." Wall Street Journal, 16 Mar. 2020, https://www.wsj.com/articles/russias-top-court-approves-plan-allowing-putin-to-stay-in-power-11584373357.

39   Kantchev, Georgi. "Russia's Top Court Approves Plan Allowing Putin to Stay in Power." Wall Street Journal, 16 Mar. 2020, https://www.wsj.com/articles/russias-top-court-approves-plan-allowing-putin-to-stay-in-power-11584373357.

the U.S. told pollsters that they had a favorable opinion of Putin, a climb of 56 net percentage points from July 2014. Nine in ten Republicans called Putin a "strong leader."[40] Remarkably, in May 2016, more people in the U.S. held a "very negative" view of Trump and Hillary Clinton than they did of Putin.[41]

Even after the 2016 election, a "surprising number of people" saw Putin "in a positive light as a man of action," Russian expert Keith Darden told the *Christian Science Monitor*.[42] And Trump strategic guru Steve Bannon urged the West to support Putin's promotion of traditional values and ideas promulgating the "underpinnings of nationalism."[43] Far-right and alt-right leaders in the U.S., including white nationalists, along with their counterparts in Europe, have also championed Putin and his rule.

Meanwhile, under the strong, savvy leadership of Xi Jinping, China has moved further away from any notions of liberal democracy—not that such a goal was ever imminent in Beijing.

---

40   Bayer, Nick. "Vladimir Putin's Popularity Is Skyrocketing Among Republicans," *Huffington Post,* December 14, 2016, http://www.huffingtonpost.com/entry/vladimir-putin-popularity-republicans_us_58518a3ce4b092f08686bd6e.

41   Zitner, Aaron and Julia Wolfe. "Trump and Clinton's Popularity Problem," *The Wall Street Journal,* May 24, 2016, http://graphics.wsj.com/elections/2016/donald-trump-and-hillary-clintons-popularity-problem/?mod=e2tw.

42   LaFranchi, Howard. "Why Putin is suddenly gaining popularity among conservatives," *The Christian Science Monitor,* December 16, 2016, http://www.csmonitor.com/USA/Politics/2016/1216/Why-Putin-is-suddenly-gaining-popularity-among-conservatives.

43   LaFranchi, Howard. "Why Putin is suddenly gaining popularity among conservatives," *The Christian Science Monitor,* December 16, 2016, http://www.csmonitor.com/USA/Politics/2016/1216/Why-Putin-is-suddenly-gaining-popularity-among-conservatives.

But under Xi, the sound one hears is of doors closing. He heads two policy coordinating bodies, the Leading Small Group for Comprehensive Deepening of Reform and the State Security Commission, which give him unparalleled power to advance his agenda. Under Xi's leadership, China has imposed greater restrictions on academic freedom,[44] tightened media controls,[45] and campaigned against "Western values" and "Western ideas" such as "Western Constitutional Democracy," freedom of the press, and human rights.[46]

Xi is a Chinese leader whose growing stature has been compared by some observers with that of Mao Zedong himself. The devotion millions of Chinese citizens and political allies seem to feel for him increasingly resembles a personality cult. Post-Mao, such overt personal glorification is officially prohibited by the Communist Party, but to Western eyes, anyway, the distinction between Xi devotion and old-fashioned Maoism is getting blurrier. Xi's speeches are broadcast from enormous TV screens in public plazas and his image is widely seen (sometimes alongside Mao's) in private homes, restaurants, and taxi cabs. Newspapers print excerpts from his speeches; highway billboards and electronic displays flash Xi slogans and aphorisms. "While there may be no 'Little Red Book' of quotations for mass con-

---

44   Li, Raymond. "Seven subjects off limits for teaching, Chinese universities told," *South China Morning Post*, May 10, 2013, http://www.scmp.com/news/china/article/1234453/seven-subjects-limits-teaching-chinese-universities-told.

45   Buckley, Chris and Andrew Jacobs, "Maoists in China, Given New Life, Attack Dissent," *New York Times*, January 4, 2015, http://www.nytimes.com/2015/01/05/world/chinas-maoists-are-revived-as-thought-police.html?_r=0.

46   McGuire, Kristian. "Xi Jinping as 'Authoritarian Reformer,'" *Freedom House*, March 3, 2015, https://freedomhouse.org/blog/xi-jinping-authoritarian-reformer.

sumption like in the bygone Mao era," writes Chris Buckley in the *New York Times*, "Mr. Xi's thinking will now infuse every aspect of party ideology in schools, the media and government agencies. In the near future, Chinese people are likely to refer to Mr. Xi's doctrines as simply 'Xi Jinping Thought,' a flattering echo of 'Mao Zedong Thought.'"[47]

Xi demands absolute loyalty to himself and to the state. He has visited China's state-run news agency, newspaper, and TV station in the same day to demand total loyalty to the Communist Party from employees. China has shut down numerous media outlets. Communist Party officials in Beijing have assumed essentially unquestioned power to control content on current-affairs and political news sites, with a special focus on critics of the regime.

A few years ago, it was possible to interpret such moves as evidence of weakness or insecurity. Xi was "worried that he will lose the rule of the Chinese Communist Party," historian Zhang Lifan said in 2016. "He is also worried that he might be replaced by his peers… For those reasons, he must hold on to his power tightly. He's like a man who doesn't know how to swim. He is going to grab hold of whatever he can."[48] Lifan's words were compelling, back then—most dictators govern at least in part through fear—but since then, Xi has removed any uncertainty about losing his grip on rule. In 2018, the National People's

---

47 Buckley, Chris. "China Enshrines 'Xi Jinping Thought,' Elevating Leader to Mao-Like Status," *The New York Times*, October 24, 2017, https://www.nytimes.com/2017/10/24/world/asia/china-xi-jinping-communist-party.html.

48 Simpson, John. "Critics fear Beijing's sharp turn to authoritarianism," *BBC News*, March 3, 2016, http://www.bbc.com/news/world-35714031.

Congress abolished presidential term limits, clearing Xi's path to ruling the country indefinitely.

Xi is remaking China in his image. He has developed a cult of personality that involves massive displays of Chinese power and his own singular authority. "There is this aristocratic flair which has now become more apparent, particularly after the military parade," said Willy Lam, referring to a grandiose military exhibition in Beijing in 2016. "The word demi-god would be an exaggeration but after the military parade he looked like an emperor."[49] Some of Xi's political allies have referred to him as "helmsman," and a newspaper called him a "great leader"— both terms associated only with Mao.[50]

Under Xi, human rights lawyers, feminists, religious leaders, and activists have faced harassment and threats of imprisonment. There is simply no room for democratic or pluralistic thought. "We have to unify the thinking and will of the whole Party first in order to unify the thinking and will of the people of all China's ethnic groups," Xi writes in *The Governance of China*.[51]

The broadest and most disturbing threat posed by the combined Russia/China axis is its open challenge to the ideals of

---

49 Phillips, Tom. "Xi Jinping: Does China Truly Love 'Big Daddy Xi' – or Fear Him?" The Guardian, 19 Sept. 2015, https://www.theguardian.com/world/2015/sep/19/xi-jinping-does-china-truly-love-big-daddy-xi-or-fear-him.

50 Wong, Chun Han. "China Celebrates Xi Jinping With Fervor Not Seen Since Mao," *The Wall Street Journal*, December 10, 2017, https://www.wsj.com/articles/china-celebrates-xi-jinping-with-fervor-not-seen-since-mao-1512907201.

51 Carlson, Benjamin. "The World According to Xi Jinping," *The Atlantic*, September 21, 2015, https://www.theatlantic.com/international/archive/2015/09/xi-jinping-china-book-chinese-dream/406387/.

democracy and its explicit formulations of alternatives models to the Western one of open societies, free markets, and democratic governance. Both China and Russia are regimes equally authoritarian and anti-Western.

Authoritarian—and Anti-Western

Anyone doubting the explicitly anti-Western nature of these two nations need only consider Xi Jinping's infamous Document No. 9, which the Central Committee of the Communist Party unveiled at Xi's behest in 2014. The document explicitly banned what it called seven core "Western values," which included "civil society," "Western constitutional democracy," and "the West's idea of journalism."

"In some respects," writes Richard Bernstein, "China resembles the old, defunct Soviet Union, as both a great power and ideological rival of the West. But China is something the world hasn't seen since the end of World War II: a dictatorial, anti-democratic power that is, unlike the Soviet Union, an economic powerhouse. And it has used its diplomatic strength to weaken the efforts of the liberal democratic countries to promote human rights while defending and protecting authoritarian practices throughout the globe."[52] Indeed, both Russia and China work together to pursue such goals.

They are getting much more aggressive in their efforts—and their efforts are greatly augmented by the American retreat

---

52 Bernstein, Richard. "China and the Rise of the New 'Authoritarian International'." RealClearInvestigations, 14 Nov. 2017, https://www.realclearinvestigations.com/articles/2017/11/12/china_and_the_authoritarian_international.html.

from confrontation and leadership, first under the Obama administration's misguided "lead from behind" strategy, and then by the Trump administration's ruinous isolationism and rejection of American global leadership.

Russia has become positively brazen in undermining democracies at home, through a host of methods including hacking, sabotage, fake news, and political destabilization. Moscow's efforts are more militarily bold when closer to home—its Ukraine destabilization activities, for example—but beyond its borders, Russia has honed and perfected an aggressive campaign of nonmilitary warfare involving a panoply of sabotage efforts. It has played upon, and helped exacerbate, the internal strife and political divisions bedeviling Western democracies. "Corruption is Putin's biggest export," says former Freedom House president David Kramer. Nations in Western Europe, including France, have been aware of Russian sabotage operations involving French elections—and of course, in the United States, Americans are now quite familiar with Russian capacities to influence American elections.

China operates more subtly, preferring to work through international institutional frameworks, where its enormous clout and economic power allow it to reshape rules, arrangements, and commitments. For example, Beijing is making a frontal assault on established information technology protocols and architecture—the better to lock in an authoritarian version of virtual technology, one that does not liberate the individual but instead empowers the state. Its censorship of discussion on its indigenous platform, WeChat, even beyond China's borders, is one example; its development of a weapon of cyberattack—dubbed the "Great Cannon"—to perpetrate denial-of-service

Internet attacks on regime critics abroad is another. And its ever-more sophisticated mastery of surveillance and control is truly chilling, especially since Beijing is increasingly finding a way to extend these tools into other countries, where they are starting to shape behavior.

Indeed, we see how, increasingly in the West, individuals and businesses with ties to China are reluctant to criticize the regime or its policies. Who can forget the sight of LeBron James, so outspoken when it comes to incidents of police brutality in the United States, staying mum on China's repression of Hong Kong protests—and his refusal to defend an NBA general manager's right to speak up about it, in the land of the free? The NBA is heavily invested in Chinese markets now; basketball is huge in the People's Republic. Without implementing anything directly or overtly—as Russia might—China uses the gravitational force of its economic might to influence behavior.

James and the NBA have plenty of company. Countless Western companies are tailoring their offerings to Chinese tastes. Even Hollywood—which has been talking about McCarthyism for 70 years—has found itself adapting to Chinese strictures, in the form of self-censorship. And American tech and finance leaders—also loud and proud in their supposed liberalism and autonomy—have applauded Xi on Chinese television, making clear that they had no intention of ruffling the regime's feathers in the form of criticism of its human rights record or challenging its confinement of self-expression. And when you add to all this the fact that President Trump has hardly been staunch in speaking out against Chinese abuses—or, more positively, speaking up on behalf of those raising their voices in protest—you understand why authoritarian countries, led by China and

Russia, feel such momentum today. Why wouldn't they, when the West, and especially America, will not reaffirm the values of liberty and freedom?

As Laura Rosenberger of the Alliance for Securing Democracy summarizes:

> The combined effect of these tactics is the weakening of democracies from within and without, and a global creep of illiberalism and authoritarianism. Russia's exploitation of internal vulnerabilities to sow division and accelerate dysfunction within Western democracies creates space for an authoritarian model. And China's increasingly assertive foreign policy, growing political and economic heft, and focus on technological development is shaping markets and governance outside its borders.[53]

"Non-Interference" as a Cover for Control

Many observers miss another key aspect of how Russia and China operate: their mutual declarations of devotion to "non-interference" in the internal affairs of other nations, which they present as respect for "sovereignty" and international law and norms. Yet these practices almost uniformly redound to the benefit of dictators. For example, early in 2019, China announced its opposition to interference in the affairs of Venezuela, which was undergoing economic crisis and political chaos,

---

53   Rosenberger, Laura. "China and Russia Are Working to Destroy Democracy, and Our Victory Is Not Assured." Dallas Morning News, 29 Sept. 2019, https://www.dallasnews.com/opinion/commentary/2019/09/29/china-and-russia-are-working-to-destroy-democracy-and-our-victory-is-not-assured/.

with skyrocketing prices, food and fuel shortages, and with a sense of impending revolution in the air.

"China supports efforts made by the Venezuelan government to protect the country's sovereignty, independence and stability," said Foreign Ministry spokeswoman Hua Chunying, calling on the factions to find a peaceful solution.[54]

It sounds admirably evenhanded, but there is much more going on here. For one thing, China and Russia tend to be loudest in their calls for non-interference in America's backyard, where, admittedly, past America interventions haven't worked out well. Their increased penetration of these enclaves has positioned them as alternative superpowers to the U.S. By standing up for Venezuelan president Nicolás Maduro, they support another autocratic ruler. And moreover, in China's case, there is blatant self-interest, as Venezuela owes China at least $20 billion in loan payments.

China and Russia determinedly resist UN sanctions against strongmen leaders, especially those aligned against the West. Preaching "non-interference" again, both vetoed Security Council sanctions against Zimbabwe's Robert Mugabe. Xi welcomed Sudanese dictator Omar Bashir with open arms to Beijing, calling him "an old friend of the Chinese people."

It is in its own Asian sphere of influence that the Chinese have made the most headway—with disturbing implications for the West. Beijing has invested billions in Cambodia, where strongman Hun Sen had previously attempted to temper his re-

---

54 "China Opposes Outside Interference in Venezuela's Affairs." Reuters, 24 Jan. 2019, https://www.reuters.com/article/us-venezuela-politics-china/china-opposes-outside-interference-in-venezuelas-affairs-idUSKCN1PI18O .

pressions to appeal to Western donors. But once Beijing flooded the country with money, Sen no longer had any need to observe niceties, cracking down on his political opponents with new impunity and praising China for giving him "no-strings support." Indeed, such support—including loans and investments—are lifelines to dictators, and China and Russia know it. Their support weakens Western efforts to press for democratic reforms and leads to more advances for anti-democratic leaders.

In Thailand, an American ally, a military coup took power from the Western-friendly, elected government, and Beijing wasted no time in forging bonds with the coup leader. That the new relationship was on strong footing became clear with a chilling detail: the Thais agreed, at Chinese request, to repatriate to China nearly 100 members of its terribly persecuted Uighur minority. Again, these efforts come wrapped in the banner of non-interference and protection of national sovereignty—but they always lead to a stronger hand for China and/or Russia.

Russia and China are taking their non-interference narrative to Western countries, too, especially in Europe, where these arguments discredit Western support for international norms and institutions by portraying it as foreign meddling. In this context, Moscow and Beijing work with a tremendous advantage: the near-total collapse of institutional legitimacy in the West, especially in institutions of government, so that arguments about non-interference increasingly fall on sympathetic ears. This is especially the case among nationalist factions in Europe—and even in the United States—which already view many national or transnational institutions with great suspicion, if not contempt. Donald Trump, after all, won the presidency by discrediting a decades-long, bipartisan consensus about international norms and the U.S. role in enforcing them—norms that tended toward the expansion of democracy. With that consensus now increasingly rejected by the public—on the left and right—non-interference is now a popular watchword. It's a great deception, but most don't see through it.

It's also crucial to understand that China and Russia's support for autocracy is not just a matter of augmenting their own power—it is also regarded as a crucial defensive strategy against the virus of democracy, against the liberal principles of the Western democracies, especially the United States. Putin, especially, has long harbored fear of Western-backed democratic revolutions—his moves into Ukraine were motivated in part by his desire to suppress an American-supported democratic movement. Moscow and Beijing have impressed upon their allies and other potential partners the dangers of engagement with the West and the many pitfalls of permitting too much popular political expression—and China, in particular, is making available its surveillance technologies to other countries so that they might more effectively spy on their citizens. To the eyes of many embattled would-be autocrats, China and Russia represent societies that run in orderly fashion, with coherent and determined political leadership.

The Revivers and Exemplars of Modern Authoritarianism

It's worth noting how historically significant Putin's Russia has been to the developments toward authoritarianism that we're seeing around the world. Though in Western media, Putin is often mocked or caricatured, his effectiveness as a leader of his country is probably unmatched in this generation, and moreover, beyond Russia's borders, he has been instrumental in developing, modeling, and disseminating some of the most important and influential anti-democratic tactics and thinking.

Putin has been instrumental in the post-Cold War rollback of human rights and liberty around the world and more broadly, in the post-Cold War discrediting of democracy as a system of government. At a time when the Fukuyama "end of history" thesis was still regarded with considerable reverence, Putin stood alone in modeling an authoritarian, nationalist vision of leadership in opposition to both the gospel of democracy as pushed by the United States—and especially against the Bush Doctrine of spreading freedom around the world—and against the globalist dream of international integration and the decline of nationhood as a defining feature of human relations. By contrast, Putin extolled Russian nationalism and identified strongman rule with Russian self-interest and Russian history—identifying himself, and his leadership, with Russia's fate, with its historical pride, and with its future. Millions of Russians responded to it.

Moreover, Putin has been a pioneer in attacking democracy as a conspiracy, and particularly in attacking Western ideals as poisons designed to undermine cultures, traditions, and social cohesion. It is in this context that one should view developments such as the Russian parliament's passage of a law to decriminalize domestic violence resulting only in "minor harm," such as bruising—a victory, proponents said, for traditional Russian family values. It's hard not to see such developments as an inverted-mirror version of the heightened awareness, in the West, about domestic violence and about women's rights more generally. Western values are anathema in Putin's Russia.

Putin has been tireless in campaigning against foreign inter-ference and contamination, and he has succeeded in discredit-ing the United States' image among millions around the world, portraying the U.S. as a dishonest broker that talks about de-mocracy but is really interested only in control.

Putin is the world's most gifted conspiracy theorist. He has, in a sense, resuscitated the era of Soviet propaganda, which al-ways warned about foreign spies and external plots to subvert the Russian government and cause internal dissension by cor-rupting public attitudes. His greatest achievement in this regard: he has persuaded millions of Russians that any pro-democratic protest movement—or anti-authoritarian protest movement, for that matter—in Russia is the product of outside plots and conspiracies, likely originating in the West. Thus Putin casts a shadow on all legitimate political criticism in Russia, and in so doing, he furnishes the pretext for aggressive action to shut down such activity. This sweeping change in public perceptions, accomplished in large part through manipulation and corrup-tion of language, is a staggering achievement—one that other autocrats around the world have learned from.

Many in the West have long labored under the illusion that modern autocrats could not control modern technologies, es-pecially the Internet and social media. Putin (and later Xi) has proved them wrong. Putin does much more, taking control of television stations, and threatening, jailing, or killing journal-ists, as he began to do during the second Chechen war.

Finally, Putin has undermined democracy by setting a new model of an anti-democratic leader who nevertheless is pop-ularly elected. Unlike Xi, for example, Putin remains in office by virtue of winning elections. These elections, of course, are widely regarded as artificial, rubber stamps for his rule, won via constitutional rejiggering, legal chicanery, and the intimidation and discrediting of potential opponents, but they are nonetheless elections—and they allow Putin to present himself as the choice of his people. He has created a paradoxical new standard: the elected president-for-life.

In short, under Putin, Russia has waged a counterrevolution against the post-Cold War consensus on democratic governance and free expression. Twenty years after taking the reins of power, Putin is still at the helm of Russia, and authoritarianism, tribalism, and nationalism have made astonishing gains in this young century, at the expense of democracy and human rights.

◆ ◆ ◆

Given its power, wealth, and reach, China is nothing less than the avatar of the global trend of authoritarianism. The combination of China's attainment of superpower status, combined with its explicit denunciation of Western democratic principles— and its elevation of its own system, via the China Dream and what it calls "socialism with Chinese characteristics"—makes it the key player in this global development.

Indeed, in the past, through the era of Mao, China was content to exercise autocratic control of its people and its regions in isolation; it did not seek to transport such systems to the rest of the world or make arguments about their relevance to other nations and peoples. Under Xi, that's changed. "The Chinese path offers a new option for other countries," Xi said at the 19th Congress of the Communist Party. "It offers Chinese wisdom and approach to solving problems facing mankind."

Other countries seem to be taking him at his word, looking to China as an alternative model of success. Indeed, while China's recent economic growth has slowed, its record over the last 30 or so years—in which it has doubled living standards about once per decade—is a daunting challenge to Western-style open markets and open societies. "Many developing countries that have introduced Western values and political systems are experiencing disorder and chaos," says Wang Jisi of Beijing University—in contrast to the Chinese model, which has provided sustained growth and stability.[55]

Some, like leaders in Ethiopia, have openly worked with Chinese officials to learn how to apply Chinese-style surveillance systems and control. The sense that Beijing has something to teach the world can also be seen in China's twenty-first-century interest in establishing alternative international institutions—such as the Asian Infrastructure and Investment Bank and the Shanghai Cooperation Organization—that operate with different principles than Western-established ones. The SCO has codified the establishment of Internet controls and censors. In a 2009 agreement among its member nations, the SCO described the dissemination of information "harmful to the spiritual, cultural, and moral spheres of other states" as a "security threat."

Authoritarianism Is Back in the Drivers' Seat

In short, thanks to the leadership of Russia and China, authoritarianism is back, a political and cultural system gaining momentum around the world. The trend toward liberal democracy

---

55 Ibid.

that seemed inevitable post-1991 now has reversed itself, with autocratic rulers and systems clearly holding the upper hand. This fact is sobering enough, but what makes it gloomier still is research demonstrating that when one or more authoritarian rulers lead major countries, more countries follow suit and become authoritarian.[56] In part, of course, this is simply the science of momentum. When the Berlin Wall came down in 1989, Western-style democracy was poised for a great growth spurt; but 40 years earlier, in the early days of the Cold War, it looked to be the Soviet Union and Red China that were gaining as the models for governance around the world. And now, in different configurations, they seem to be doing so again.

It's clear that the global order, which for so long looked to be trending toward democratic government and expansion of political liberty and human rights, now faces an unprecedented threat—or at least, a threat more formidable than at any time since the outset of the Cold War. This threat is magnified by signs that Russia and China want to expand their vision and reach. For most of the early years of the twenty-first century, as Russia began moving against democracy and China consolidated its totalitarian hold on its people, observers could console themselves that these two autocracies did not seek to bring these systems beyond their borders. It's much harder to believe that now.

After all, how can any American believe it, knowing what we know about Russian interference in the 2016 presidential election? That episode stands as chilling evidence that Moscow is

---

56   Kendall-Taylor, Andrea, and David Shullman. "How Russia and China Undermine Democracy." Foreign Affairs, https://www.foreignaffairs.com/articles/china/2018-10-02/how-russia-and-china-undermine-democracy.

willing to pursue efforts to destabilize the politics of the United States. And let us remember, too, that the goal of these efforts was in fact accomplished: regardless of what effect Russian cyber-hacking had on the actual voting, it *has* clearly destabilized American politics. And if the Russians are willing to try such audacious things against a superpower like the U.S., they are surely even bolder when it comes to weaker countries. Other European countries, notably France, report Russian attempts at similar electoral sabotage. More broadly, the rise of populist, nationalist demagogues across Europe is more evidence that the Putin model has broadened appeal.

In a time of historic technological innovation, autocracies are pioneering new methods of surveillance and popular repression. China's social credit system—what Freedom House calls, aptly, "digital totalitarianism"—would empower the state to gather broad-ranging data on citizens and use it to build a profile in which citizens are "scored" based on their perceived "trustworthiness." Chinese Communist officials claims that the social credit system will soon "allow the trustworthy to roam everywhere under heaven while making it hard for the discredited to take a single step."[57] How might one become discredited? By disseminating banned ideas or opinions, participating in political protests, or other disallowed activities involving free expression or political dissidence.

It all adds up to a tide moving in entirely the wrong direction: authoritarian gains, democratic setbacks. The global

---

57 Mistreanu, Simina. "Life Inside China's Social Credit Laboratory." Foreign Policy, 3 Apr. 2018, https://foreignpolicy.com/2018/04/03/life-inside-chinas-social-credit-laboratory/.

balance of power has been shifting between democracy and autocracy for about a decade now, as Freedom House has tirelessly chronicled. In 2018, for the 13th year in a row, Freedom House's annual survey showed a decline in global freedom. "The reversal has spanned a variety of countries in every region," the organization's report declares, "from long-standing democracies like the United States to consolidated authoritarian regimes like China and Russia. The overall losses are still shallow compared with the gains of the late 20th century, but the pattern is consistent and ominous. Democracy is in retreat."[58] The most troubling sign is the decline in liberty in democratic countries. For the Freedom House authors, most concerning of all was the retreat that the United States seemed to be making, under the Trump administration, from its traditional role as defender of democracy around the world. Indeed, the U.S. no longer prioritizes democracy promotion as a key component of its foreign policy. And under Trump, the United States shows no sign of elevating human rights as a priority, either.

Is the democratic model in genuine decline, worldwide? The *Journal of Democracy* sees three reasons to worry: the economic and political instability in advanced democracies; a new self-confidence of some authoritarian countries; and a general shift in the geopolitical balance between democracies and their rivals, as the Freedom House data show.[59]

---

58 "Freedom in the World 2019: Democracy in Retreat." Freedom House, 2019, https://freedomhouse.org/report/freedom-world/2019/democracy-retreat.

59 Plattner, Marc F. "Is Democracy in Decline?" *Journal of Democracy*, January 2015, http://www.journalofdemocracy.org/sites/default/files/Plattner-26-1.pdf.

And the energies of the Russia/China axis are not just driven toward preserving their own power or fostering authoritarian rule around the world. In their focus and in their commitment to these systems of anti-democratic governance, they are explicitly and aggressively anti-Western. They see the West, with its dream of liberal democracy, as the fundamental enemy. They are not simply revanchist but aggressive.

We need to realize that we're at a new point in history. Authoritarianism is not only back, it may be stronger, in terms of its political resiliency, than at any time before. "Variations on the systems that have proved effective in suppressing political dissent and pluralism in Russia and China are less likely to collapse than traditional authoritarian states," as Freedom House warns, "given their relative flexibility and pragmatism." As the organization goes on to describe, the two latter-day authoritarian standard-bearers have proved themselves adept at navigating economic downturns and other political tumults that, in the past, more commonly brought down autocratic regimes. And Freedom House sees more efforts, not less, by authoritarian states, especially Russia and China, in the future to "influence the political choices and government polices of democracies," warning that these efforts will "become increasingly difficult to control due to global economic integration, new developments in the delivery of propaganda, and sympathetic leaders and political movements within the democracies."

I wish I could say that these assessments are too grim, but I concur with them wholeheartedly—and indeed, I have been making similar warnings for years now. "Putin and his cohorts have learned well how to use democratic openness against democracy itself," Freedom House warns, and here, too, they see the issue clearly. In the Western democracies, we have seen a disturbing growth of sympathy for authoritarianism and nationalism over the last decade—mostly from the Right. Meantime, on the Left, there is a corresponding contempt for constitutional and cultural traditions, a disdain for the very ideas of freedom and democracy, in favor of an obsessive identity politics that, in its own way, is simply a variation of the tribalism seen on the Right.

And worst of all, the United States, the global standard-bearer for democratic governance and individual liberty, is led by a president who himself seems to share some of the authoritarian traits of Putin and Xi—and, indeed, who often speaks of them in flattering terms. Whatever the future holds, of one thing we may be certain: unless and until the United States of America recommits itself to democracy at home and to the defense of democracy and human rights abroad, the march of authoritarianism will continue—perhaps all the way into "a new dark age," as Churchill called it.

CHAPTER THREE

The New Battle for the Pacific: China vs. America

T HE SOLOMON ISLANDS, A SOVEREIGN STATE OF SIX MAJOR islands and hundreds of smaller ones in the southeast Asia Pacific, doesn't make a lot of news, but in September 2019 it did, when its government announced that it had voted to withdraw diplomatic recognition from Taiwan and establish official ties with the People's Republic of China. Political leaders in the Solomons had decided that it could no longer resist the gravitational lure of Chinese offers for large-scale investment. To accept, however, required breaking off with Taipei, and in doing so, the Solomons lowered the number of countries still recognizing Taiwan to 16. A few days later, that number dropped to 15, as the island nation of Kiribati switched to the China column as well.

For longtime supporters of Taiwan, these moves were the latest dispiriting developments in a long-running story of declining recognition for the democratic country. But they also signified something much larger: the latest setback in the United States' struggle against China's mounting diplomatic influence in the Pacific region, an influence that Beijing augments not only with its massive economic presence but also, increasingly, with a military and naval buildup that menaces powerful neighboring countries from Japan to the Philippines, coerces smaller and weaker ones—like the Solomons and Kiribati—into Beijing's orbit, and puts in question the future of a region once safely patrolled and dominated by the United States. It is an open contest now in the Pacific between Washington and Beijing, one in which the Chinese have made such rapid inroads so that the window in which America could have halted its penetrations has already closed.

Put simply, the United States is losing the battle for power and influence in the Pacific to China. We are being bested politically, diplomatically, economically, and—soon enough—militarily, as China builds the world's largest navy and prepares itself for confrontation with the United States by developing sophisticated, offensive missile and rocket systems as well as defense and detection technologies.

"The military balance in the Pacific is going in the wrong direction," says Elbridge Colby, until recently a former deputy assistant secretary of defense for strategy and force development. "The scale of the Chinese military buildup is so significant and so advanced that we need to use every potential arrow in our quiver."[60]

------

60 Seligman, Lara. "Trump's Plan to Leave a Major Arms Treaty With Russia Might Actually Be About China." Foreign Policy, 22 Oct. 2018, https://foreignpolicy.com/2018/10/22/trumps-plan-to-leave-a-major-arms-treaty-with-russia-might-actually-be-about-china/.

"We have never encountered an Asian country as powerful as China is now, let alone as powerful as it will likely become in the decades ahead," writes Hugh White, author of *The China Choice*.[61]

It is not just that the United States needs to revamp its defense posture or deal more effectively, from alliances to diplomacy, with allies and potential allies in the region; more broadly, as in other areas, the problem is the lack of any coherent strategy for how to deal with China's rise and penetration in the Pacific. We're running out of time to get it right.

The Chinese Power Buildup

"The task of building a powerful navy has never been as urgent as it is today," said Xi Jinping in April 2018, as he watched naval exercises, the largest in the history of the People's Republic, off the island of Hainan. China has acted accordingly: The People's Republic now boasts the world's largest navy, with its warships and submarines outnumbering those of the United States, which has cut its active ship count in half since a Reagan-era peak of 594 in 1987.[62] Though experts say that the American fleet remains superior in quality, the Chinese are overcoming that disadvantage through sheer numbers. Beijing is preparing for "a limited military conflict from the sea," according to an assessment in *The Science of Military Strategy*, a military journal.

———

61 White, Hugh. "Australia Must Prepare for a Chinese Military Base in the Pacific." The Guardian, 14 July 2019, https://www.theguardian.com/world/commentis-free/2019/jul/15/australia-must-prepare-for-a-chinese-military-base-in-the-pacific.

62 "US Ship Force Levels." Naval History and Heritage Command, www.history.navy.mil/research/histories/ship-histories/us-ship-force-levels.html.

Though China began expanding its navy 20 years ago, Xi has aggressively accelerated the effort since taking power in 2013. It is important to understand that Beijing's naval buildup has not just military and economic components but also historical and cultural ones. One of Xi's consistent themes is that China's naval expansion will help turn the page on what the Chinese Communists regard as a period of historical humiliation in the nineteenth and early twentieth centuries, when China lacked power on the seas and was vulnerable to the control of European imperial powers and Japan. "Every Chinese school child learns that China's suffering arose partly because of the lack of a modern navy," a Reuters investigative report observes. "Infamously, in the final years of the Qing Dynasty, the Empress Dowager diverted funds earmarked for naval modernization to building a new Summer Palace. This contributed to China's heavy defeat in the 1894-95 war with Japan, in which a rising Japanese navy smashed the Chinese fleet."[63] The desire to overcome and eradicate this history of subjugation is a powerful psychological tool for the Chinese leadership in Beijing.

As part of his dramatic seizure of control and command over the state military apparatus—a power he now wields more absolutely than any Chinese leader since Mao—Xi has sharpened his focus on naval priorities. He has purged corrupt generals and sought to divert resources from the Chinese army toward naval, air, and missile forces—that is, toward the Pacific.

In April 2018, China launched its first-ever aircraft carrier, the *Liaoning*, which originated as a Soviet ship in the late 1980s

---

63   Lague, David, and Benjamin Kang Lim. "China's Vast Fleet Is Tipping the Balance in the Pacific." Reuters, 30 Apr. 2019, https://www.reuters.com/investigates/special-report/china-army-navy/.

and was then purchased, after the fall of the Soviet Union, by a Chinese investor under the ruse that China would convert it to floating casino. All along, however, Beijing intended it for naval use.[64] The ship has been declared "combat ready," and its battle group regularly circles Taiwan.

More aircraft carriers—these to be made in China, and with more advanced technology than the *Liaoning* possesses—are in development, perhaps reaching a total of five or six. With each new project, China moves its naval arsenal forward, even though it continues to work from older Soviet designs and often using Soviet military hardware.

These plans reflect Xi's priorities of shifting China's defense efforts and resources from the People's Liberation Army (PLA) to the buildout of what Beijing hopes will become a "Blue Water Navy," the cherished goal of superpowers—a naval force capable of operating globally, across the earth's vast oceans. Though other nations, France and Britain among them, make claims to this status, the global standard-bearer remains the United States Navy, and it is the U.S. that Beijing has in mind as a benchmark—and a target.

In addition to the aircraft carriers, China has expanded its naval assets in other areas, too, and on a scale few other nations could even contemplate. Beijing has introduced a new class of destroyers, called "super destroyers," that U.S. naval experts consider on par with modern warships manufactured in the West. In the last decade alone, Beijing has put an additional

---

64 Myers, Steven L. "With Ships and Missiles, China Is Ready to Challenge U.S. Navy in Pacific." The New York Times, 29 Aug. 2018, https://www.nytimes.com/2018/08/29/world/asia/china-navy-aircraft-carrier-pacific.html.

100 warships and submarines into service—an increase that exceeds the total naval fleets of most other countries. The rapid ramp-up of submarine production is especially striking. In the mid-1990s, China built only three new submarines, but today it has 45-50 "modern" subs and plans to keep making more.

All told, it adds up to a new global naval champion, at least in terms of sheer numbers: in 2019, China's warships and submarines totaled about 400, compared with 288 for the United States.[65]

And yet, those numbers barely tell the story of what China is up to in the Pacific, with its naval buildup. It's not just about ships or subs but also about technology, capabilities—and strategies. In all these areas, what China is up to is both breathtakingly ambitious and profoundly disconcerting.

Consider the missile technologies that Beijing is deploying as part of its rapid advances in what analysts call "asymmetrical weaponry," including radar, satellites, and missiles, to erode the advantage of America's superior aircraft carriers. In this area, the focus is on China's expanding capacity for "anti-access/area denial," or what military experts call A2/AD for short. The best definition I've seen of A2/AD for laypeople was offered by Luis Simón, a professor at the Institute for European Studies, who defines it as "that family of military capabilities used to prevent or constrain the deployment of opposing forces into a given theater of operations and reduce their freedom of maneuver

65   Lague, David, and Benjamin Kang Lim. "China's Vast Fleet Is Tipping the Balance in the Pacific." Reuters, 30 Apr. 2019, https://www.reuters.com/investigates/special-report/china-army-navy/.

once in a theater."[66] The Chinese prefer to call it "counter-intervention," a telling phrase, as it reflects their belief that they have the right to expand their interests in the Pacific by any means necessary—and that any forces, including those of the United States, that aim to thwart those incursions are invaders who must be repelled.

To understand the significance of China's technological advances in the Pacific, and why A2/AD capabilities are so crucial, it's important to understand what Elbridge Colby, a former director of the defense program at the Center for a New American Security, calls "fait accompli" logic, which he sees facing the United States increasingly when it deals with its two key adversaries—whether it's Russia's seizure of the Crimea or China's expansion of its Pacific influence and colonization of Pacific islands for military and economic purposes. Fait accompli logic, Colby says, involves an aggressor "seizing territory before the defender and its patron can react sufficiently and then making sure that the counterattack needed to eject it would be so risky, costly, and aggressive that the United States would balk at mounting it."[67]

That's precisely what A2/AD enables the Chinese to do in Pacific. A key component is an expanding arsenal of high-speed ballistic missiles, which can strike moving naval vessels. American military planners are particularly concerned about the new classes that China has developed, the DF-21D and the DF-26,

---

66   Simon, Luis. "DEMYSTIFYING THE A2/AD BUZZ." War on the Rocks, 4 Jan. 2017, https://warontherocks.com/2017/01/demystifying-the-a2ad-buzz/.

67   Colby, Elbridge. "HOW TO WIN AMERICA'S NEXT WAR." Foreign Policy, 5 May 2019, https://foreignpolicy.com/2019/05/05/how-to-win-americas-next-war-china-russia-military-infrastructure/.

which they call "carrier killers." Yes—ballistic missiles that can strike the pride of the American fleet.

It's not just the range of such missiles—the DF-26 may be able to reach as far as American ships and bases in Guam—that is so alarming. They are also regarded by American officials as nearly impossible to detect and intercept. That means that the United States, to deter them, would not be able to rely, as it so often has in the past, on its superior technological ability to shoot down enemy missile strikes. Instead, it would have to neutralize the missiles before they were fired—by making a direct strike inside Chinese territory. And that, of course, would come with extraordinary risks that pertain to any serious escalation with a major military power.

Thus, the DF-21 and DF-26 may exert a kind of paralyzing, deterrent effect on American options in the Pacific—precisely as the Chinese intend. "The U.S. Navy has not previously faced a threat from highly accurate ballistic missiles capable of hitting moving ships at sea," read a report issued to Congress in 2019, referring to the new missiles as "game-changing."

Armed with such capabilities, the Chinese will be much tougher to dislodge from their increasingly aggressive posture in the Pacific, where Beijing has been throwing its weight around for years around various island chains, including those over the Paracel, Spratly, and Senkaku island chains, in all of which it is engaged in contentious disputes with its Pacific neighbors—and has resented the presence of United States naval forces, patrolling to ensure free passage in international waters.

Beijing has been flexing its muscles in these disputes for years, but its provocations grow ever more brazen, and they seem to carry the implicit message of mounting Chinese confidence that the Americans cannot stop them. Chinese warships have never been more active than they are now in the waters off these disputed islands, and the world's largest navy is becoming increasingly confident, and adept, at repelling American attempts to impose order. Chinese ships have not hesitated to confront American and Australian vessels approaching the island chains. As the Americans and Australians see it, they're enforcing freedom of the seas; as China sees it, they're engaging in a "a provocative act."

Another factor in the fait accompli scenario is nukes. China is the world's third-ranking nuclear power, behind the United States and Russia. It has 228 confirmed nuclear missiles, though the full extent of the arsenal is anyone's guess, since China, unlike the United States and Russia, is party to no nuclear arms agreements and thus faces no requirements for testing or verification. The nukes are particularly potent in the equation when considered in the context of the shrunken American naval fleet and how overstretched its current resources are.

Consider, for example, as Mark Helprin did for the *Wall Street Journal*, what happens if China were to attack American bases in Japan, South Korea, or Guam. If successful in these strikes—if, in other words, the attacks effectively took out the bases—the only proportionate American response would be an attack on Chinese bases. But such attacks, as Helprin rightly observes, "would raise the specter of nuclear escalation." Unless the United States were willing to face that scenario, the Chinese would effectively "banish the U.S. from its environs, condemning us to a long-distance campaign to which the U.S. Navy in its present state—overstretched, undertrained and half the size of the Reagan Navy—is inadequate."[68]

---

68   https://www.wsj.com/articles/the-u-s-is-ceding-the-pacific-to-china-11551649516

And Helprin doesn't see the fait accompli logic necessarily ending at the Pacific, either. He envisions scenarios in which China uses its superior forces to "block the southern capes and choke points east of Suez," knowing that "it would have to contend only with roughly half of our already diminished fleets." And China's increased foothold in the Panama Canal zone— which the United States has unconscionably let happen—means a similar logic could apply there, too, in America's own backyard. (I'll have more to say about China's investments in Latin America and its cultivation of the region's political leaders in Chapter 7.)

And there's still more: China's new J-20 stealth fighter, though apparently behind on its production numbers, "has been commissioned into the air force's combat service," Beijing's Defense Ministry says.[69] Though some critics question whether the J-20 can truly stack up against the American F-22 or F-35 stealth fighters, there is no question that the jet represents a breaking of the stealth monopoly previously held by the United States and Japan in the Pacific. There is now a new player on the scene. The Chinese are also conducting flights of their strategic bomber, the H-6, to demonstrate, the Pentagon believes, Chinese capability to strike American bases in Japan and South Korea. The H-6, it is also believed, could use airfields in the Spratlys or the Paracels to conduct attacks across Southeast Asia.

All these capabilities make American options for such disputes more constrained, because A2/AD capacities mean that America cannot act with impunity. Moreover, A2/AD also en-

---

69 Keck, Zachary. "Sorry China, But The J-20 Can't Beat America's F-22 Or F-35 Stealth Fighters." The National Interest, 7 Jan. 2020, https://nationalinterest.org/blog/buzz/sorry-china-j-20-cant-beat-americas-f-22-or-f-35-stealth-fighters-111541.

sures that China does not need to engage the Americans in a frontal conflict—and in fact can avoid having one—because the technologies allow it simply to protect the gains it has already made and the penetrations it has already advanced. For the Pentagon, aggressive attempts to move Beijing out of a certain area will resemble a high-stakes gamble, not worth the potential price. The Chinese presence will become a fait accompli.

"China is now capable of controlling the South China Sea in all scenarios short of war with the United States," says Admiral Philip S. Davidson, commander of the United States Indo-Pacific Command. Pointing to China's growing technological sophistication and asymmetrical capabilities, he told the U.S. Senate that "There is no guarantee that the United States would win a future conflict with China."

Think about those words. They reflect a judgment still relatively recent, but increasingly unquestioned. The Pacific is no longer an American sphere of influence. It is the site of a great superpower struggle, one in which the rival superpower holds more and more of the cards.

And it holds those Pacific cards not only in the air and on the sea, but under the water. The Chinese have also been aggressively pursuing undersea assets in the Pacific—including those currently controlled by the United States.

Consider what's happening around the 1,000-square-kilometer Mariana Islands chain in the northwestern Pacific, which comprises the Commonwealth of the Northern Mariana Islands and Guam. The islands—just five hours from Beijing—are U.S. controlled and long regarded as a crucial harness point for American power and influence in the region. Two U.S. military bases are located on Guam, taking up more than a quarter of its land area, and Guam residents serve in the military in much higher proportions than the residents of any U.S. state. The U.S. has installed an anti-ballistic missile system on the island as well; it has put another in South Korea. Up until recently, the region was often referred to as "the American lake" or "Australia's backyard," but now Beijing is making incursions, especially beneath the waves, along the western edge of what is known as the Mariana Trench, the deepest point on Earth.

What's Beijing after with its undersea exploration? Its operation of unpiloted gliders at depths of 7,000 meters—about 23,000 feet—appears to be driven by the desire to help the PLA's submarine fleet in its antidetection efforts. The goal: a globally operating submarine fleet, one that can navigate undetected, certainly across the Pacific, from Japan, Taiwan, and the Philippines to the Marianas.

"China is running research vessels everywhere," said Lyle Goldstein, director of the China Maritime Studies Institute at the U.S. Naval War College. "One major impetus is for economic development. On the other hand, there are strong military and strategic reasons to pursue this course. China understands there is a very wide crossover between military and civilian technology when it comes to oceanography."[70]

Everywhere the U.S. looks in the Pacific, it sees Beijing staring back. And the more U.S. analysts and security officials evaluate the new terms, the more they come to a grim conclusion: the U.S. has not just lost any chance to slow Chinese expansion

---

70 Tobin, Meaghan. "US-China Battle for Dominance Extends across Pacific, above and below the Sea." South China Morning Post, 19 Jan. 2019, https://www.scmp.com/week-asia/geopolitics/article/2182752/us-china-battle-dominance-extends-across-pacific-above-and.

in the Pacific. In the broader battle for Pacific supremacy, China is poised to win.

Why China Is Poised to Win

What knowledgeable observers have concluded is that the Chinese have achieved enormous momentum for their efforts in the Pacific, can absorb defense spending increases as a portion of GDP more effectively than the United States, and moreover, have the political unity of purpose that the Americans clearly do not. Beijing can continue strengthening its hand in the Pacific—as the American hand weakens.

The United States has seen its power eroded by multiple factors. Certainly, our political dysfunction should be placed near the top of the list. Given the monumental nature of the Chinese challenge in the Pacific, a unified America would face a daunting enough task; but an America as divided and polarized as it is today simply cannot marshal the political will or resources to formulate a compelling strategy, win the necessary support to implement it, and generate the needed funds to make it happen.

The United States is also stretched in ways that Beijing is not. Washington is reeling from nearly 20 years of continuous war in the Middle East, with staggering financial and human losses and little tangible gain. To command the same kind of resources for the Pacific challenge seems remote. The Pentagon endured years of budget austerity, in part due to a damaging "sequester" during the Obama years, before President Trump ramped up spending again. One of the many casualties of under-investment has been the advanced capabilities that the Chinese have so diligently cultivated.

These factors and others were considered in a comprehensive and sobering 2019 report by the University of Sydney's United States Study Center, entitled "Averting Crisis: American strategy, military spending and collective defense in the Indo-Pacific," though its findings belie that somewhat hopeful title. "America no longer enjoys military primacy in the Indo-Pacific and its capacity to uphold a favorable balance of power is increasingly uncertain," the authors observe, and they seem to be choosing their words carefully, almost as if to soften the blow. One emerges from reading the report, not with the feeling that America's capacity to uphold a favorable balance of power is more dubious than uncertain.

The report's Australian authors see what others see in the Pacific: that the Chinese have made substantial enough incursions to keep the Americans from rolling back any of their gains—let alone effectively challenging them when they make new attempts. "Having studied the American way of war—premised on power projection and all-domain military dominance—China has deployed a formidable array of precision missiles and other counter-intervention systems to undercut America's military primacy," they write. "By making it difficult for US forces to operate within range of these weapons, Beijing could quickly use limited force to achieve a *fait accompli* victory—particularly around Taiwan, the Japanese archipelago or maritime Southeast Asia—before America can respond."[71]

---

71 O'Connor, Tom. "China May Win Fight 'Before America Can Respond' in Pacific, Report Says." Newsweek, 19 Aug. 2019, https://www.newsweek.com/china-win-america-pacific-1455065.

The Australian analysts see Taiwan—whose independence has been a defining issue for U.S.-China relations since 1949—as particularly vulnerable to the fait accompli scenario. Perhaps Beijing does not need a full-scale invasion of Taiwan to accomplish its objectives of retaking control over the longtime holdout to Communist dominance. Perhaps a "limited war" would suffice, since even a limited war would require so much from the United States to stop it. Likewise, the disputed island chains might be secured for Chinese dominance with a combination of tools, from asymmetrical to cyber, that alleviate the need for a conventional-war showdown with the U.S. The key: China now has such formidable conventional-war capabilities that the U.S. knows how high the price would be if it were to try to engage it—thus, the lesser tools might accomplish the same objectives. "In all these scenarios," they write, "Beijing's aim would be to strike first to secure longstanding political goals or strategically valuable objectives before the United States can do anything to stop it."

In short, the United States is operating with an obsolete mindset. Though it faces the challenge from a superpower in the Pacific, that superpower is not approaching the confrontation in the conventional way—as a potential clash between great armies and navies. Instead, it is using a full array of tools and strategies to remind the U.S. of its force and capability and putting American planners persistently on the defensive.

But perhaps the most sobering finding in the report is its analysis of what might happen should that superpower clash of great militaries occur. In this scenario, the United States would face grim prospects:

Asymmetries in power, time, distance and interest would all work against an effective American response. Under present-day U.S. posture in the region, most American and allied bases and forward-deployed ships, troops and aircraft would struggle to survive a PLA salvo attack, and would be initially forced to focus on damage limitation rather than blunting the thrust of a Chinese offensive.

American forces that are able to operate would be highly constrained in the early phases of a crisis—lacking air and naval dominance, outnumbered by their PLA equivalents and severely challenged by the loss of enabling infrastructure, like functioning airstrips, fuel depots and port facilities, all of which would be at least temporarily degraded by precision strikes.[72]

We Need a Strategy

Underlying everything is the fact that the United States doesn't have a coherent strategy for combating China's surge in the Pacific theater. And, to hear President Trump talk about it, we barely need one. "We have the strongest military in the world right now," Trump has boasted. "Right now, there's nobody that's even close to us militarily—not even close." With his typical bluster, the president dismissed concerns about Chinese power and aggression in the Pacific. "They'd pay a price they wouldn't want to pay." What Trump seems unwilling to admit or recognize is how much the Chinese have already achieved.

---

72 Wolfgang, Ben. "China Could Crush U.S. Military in Pacific: Report." The Washington Times, 20 Aug. 2019, https://www.washingtontimes.com/news/2019/aug/20/china-could-crush-us-military-pacific-report/.

Fortunately, though, there are signs that Washington might be waking from its slumber and beginning to try to address the situation. In its Indo-Pacific Strategy report of 2019, the Pentagon prioritized containing Chinese expansion and strengthening alliances and partnerships with allies in the region. "China is the priority," said General Robert Brown, the U.S. Pacific commander. Brown says that the U.S. will increase troop rotations in the region and step up military exercises, including its Pacific Pathways exercise, which involves Japan, Indonesia, and Malaysia. Most promisingly, the Pentagon wants to invest in land-based hypersonic missiles—a new class of weapon that can travel 1,000 miles, perhaps farther, while moving at the speed of sound.

Still, these efforts are not nearly enough. There is no substitute for an American strategy that embraces as its central principle a reorientation of the military balance of power in the Pacific. Anything short of that is not going to get the job done. Mark Helprin sketches out a clear picture of what we face:

> China has medium-range ballistic missiles, air-launched land-attack cruise missiles, air-refueled bombers and fighter bombers, sea-based missiles, and seaborne commandos. To protect our bases from all this we need long-range anti-ship missiles, adequately defended, on outpost islands; deep, reinforced aircraft shelters rather than surface revetments and flimsy hangars; multilayered missile and aircraft defenses in numbers sufficient to meet saturation attacks; deeply sheltered command and control, runway repair, munitions, and stores; and radically strengthened base defense

against infantry, special forces, and sabotage. It would
be expensive, but essential.[73]

I'm heartened by the fact that the Pentagon is taking steps
that suggest awareness of the problems in the Pacific, but everything is moving too slow. At the pace our realization is growing,
we're just not going to be able to make a difference in the calculus before it's too late. China is constantly seeking to heighten
tensions in the region, both between itself and its neighbors and
between those neighbors and the United States.

The coronavirus crisis has not slowed these efforts down
whatsoever; if anything, it has magnified them. Since Covid-19
was declared a global pandemic in March 2020, China has continued to involve itself in incidents in the region, including
sending PLA aircraft across an unofficial demarcation line in
the Taiwan Strait, in a clear probe for a reaction (Taiwan scrambled aircraft); chasing a Vietnamese fishing vessel and causing
it to sink after hitting some rocks in the South China Sea; and
sending one of its own fishing vessels into a collision with a
Japanese destroyer, an incident that may be the latest involving
China's "Little Blue Men" or "maritime militia," described by
the Pentagon as "an armed reserve force of civilians available
for mobilization" that involves itself in "coercive activities to
achieve China's political goals without fighting."[74]

---

73 Helprin, Mark. "The U.S. Is Ceding the Pacific to China." Wall Street Journal,
3 Mar. 2019, https://www.wsj.com/articles/the-u-s-is-ceding-the-pacific-to-chi-
na-11551649516.

74 Denmark, Abraham, et al. "SAME AS IT EVER WAS: CHINA'S PANDEMIC
OPPORTUNISM ON ITS PERIPHERY." War on the Rocks, 16 Apr. 2020, https://
warontherocks.com/2020/04/same-as-it-ever-was-chinas-pandemic-opportunism-
on-its-periphery/.

Another huge factor here, also not amenable to slow time-frames, is the mounting risk that China, through its massive and seemingly bottomless capacity for economic investment, will continue peeling off U.S. allies in the region. Its determination to reduce the number of nations recognizing Taiwan is one example of this. The more these allies, especially smaller ones, see the United States as weakened and China as the growing power in the area, the less motivation they will have not only to stand with Taiwan but also to maintain the kinds of investments they need to make to fulfill commitments under their alliance with the United States. And once those pieces start to wobble, and fall, and the U.S. Pacific alliance is seen as shaky or dissolving, there will be no turning back.

China has been tireless and determined in making its play in the Pacific, across all these fronts. The United States' response has been catastrophically inadequate. There is no point in trying to soften the assessment or hedge the stakes: without swift and dramatic reversal of current trends, America will lose the Pacific.

CHAPTER FOUR

The New Middle East: Russia In, America Out

E VEN BY THE STANDARDS OF THE MODERN MIDDLE EAST, IT was a stunning turn of events. On January 3, 2020, a drone strike ordered by President Trump killed major general Qasem Soleimani, commander of Iran's Islamic Revolutionary Guard and by some accounts the second most powerful man in that country, next to supreme leader Ayatollah Khamenei. It was Soleimani who had masterminded and overseen Tehran's mountingly successful efforts to expand its influence in the Middle East through networks of terrorist operatives and proxies. Soleimani was also the commander of the Quds Force, deemed a terrorist organization by the United States. One American columnist described Soleimani as "Iran's Patton." Though the strike killed nine others, including Abu Mahdi al-Muhandis, commander of Kata'ib Hezbollah, the directed killing of Soleimani garnered most of the attention. It was regarded, by some, as an act of war.

The strikes had originated as an American response to increasing Iranian provocations. In the waning days of 2019, Kata'ib Hezbollah rocket attacks on an air base in Iraq, housing both American and Iraqi troops, killed an American contractor. The U.S. responded with airstrikes that killed more than two dozen members of Katai'ib Hezbollah. In turn, Shia militiamen organized a riot outside the U.S. embassy in Iraq's Green Zone—invoking memories of the Iranian hostage crisis, which started with an attack on the American embassy. This episode was contained, and the rioters did not penetrate the gates.

Trump had had enough, however, and after reviewing less dramatic options, decided to take out Soleimani. It was a potentially historic moment, as Trump's action clearly went well beyond the carefully calibrated counterattacks familiar to past administrations. The strike was brilliantly planned and executed.

While Trump supporters on the American Right cheered it, more skeptical observers rightly saw the killing of Soleimani as disturbing, even confounding. It was yet another instance of Trump's erratic foreign policy approach, one that seems to rely as much on impulse as on analysis. Consider how Trump had run for president by railing against America's "endless wars," especially those in the Middle East; now he had taken a dramatic strike against Iran, one that seemed to put the United States on the brink of a new conflict in the region. And as if to prepare for that eventuality, Trump deployed at least 3,000 American troops to the Middle East. And he did all this as the result of a strike that he had ordered without congressional approval.

Critics of the strike were not mourning Soleimani. Few, if any commentators lamented the demise of the Iranian general, with his long career of mayhem and brutality. What was at issue was the consequences of the strike: had the United States just initiated a huge escalation in hostilities with Iran? And what did Trump's removal of Soleimani mean for the region's balance of power, and America's role within it?

For now, the first question goes unanswered. Fears of an all-out war have not materialized, though the Middle East is a region with a long memory, and the United States should not delude itself about Iranian willingness to exact revenge, somewhere down the line. We have not heard the last of this. As for the second question: despite Trump's self-congratulatory tweeting about the attack, and the cheering of pro-Trump conservatives, I'm afraid that the Soleimani strike does not change much, in terms of who holds the most powerful hand in the region.

The sobering fact remains that the preeminent power in the Middle East is no longer the United States but Russia, under the leadership of Vladimir Putin. Why? Because the United States has conceded leadership in the Middle East to Putin. One-offs, like the killing of Soleimani, won't change that.

The American Retreat

Ever since the debacle of the Iraq War, a disaster whose effects continue to play out in American foreign policy, the United States has been on the back foot in the Middle East. In 2008, when Barack Obama won the presidency, he did so by running explicitly against the Iraq War and George W. Bush's foreign policy. Obama's approach involved the elevation of "soft power"—non-military assertions of American strength, whether diplomatic or economic or rhetorical, designed to make other nations or groups identify with American objectives, or at least recognize their self-interest in doing so. Soft power, of course, has always been around, and the American version of it has done great things in the world; look no further than the Marshall Plan. But soft power works best when it is backed by hard power, and in the Obama years, U.S. reluctance to use hard power gradually became apparent to our adversaries. They understood that they could act against American interests with little fear of reprisal. The attack on the American consulate in Benghazi, Libya, resulting in the death of the American ambassador there, was one example. Syria's use of chemical weapons against rebel forces in Damascus, violating Obama's stated "red line" for U.S. military action, was another—because Obama walked back his threat of intervention and chose to do nothing. Obama's red-line fiasco set a new standard for United States passivity in the Middle East; for the rest of his time in office, he was reacting to events there, not shaping them.

Donald Trump, meantime, took the United States' retreat from leadership to a new level. Trump spoke the language of power and force—he loved to threaten foes with destruction at the hands of America's "great military"—but his deepest wish, regarding the Middle East, was to get the hell out. He had run for president, after all, by campaigning against "endless wars," and he had broken the long-running silence in the Republican Party about the Iraq War, openly declaring it a disaster. The most dramatic reflection of Trump's priorities was his announcement, in autumn 2019, that the United States was withdrawing its military forces from Syria. The U.S. would step aside and endorse a Turkish effort to move against Kurdish forces near the Syrian border. The Turks had long sought such an opportunity, viewing the Kurdish forces as a terrorist insurgency.

But these Kurdish forces had been the most reliable and loyal United States partners in the region. As part of the Syrian Democratic Forces, they had fought alongside Americans in battling the Islamic State. Now Trump was leaving them to their own devices against a much stronger foe that had been set on their destruction for years.

It didn't take long for the consequences of this decision to play out. Turkish forces, along with the Turkish-backed Free Syrian Army, pushed into northeastern Syria within days of Trump's announcement, bombing and shelling territory held by Syrian Kurds of the Syrian Democratic Forces, who had allied themselves with Washington. A Turkish ground offensive soon followed.

In his usual way, Trump portrayed the decision as common-sensical and in the interests of the United States. "The Kurds fought with us," he wrote on Twitter, "but were paid massive amounts of money and equipment to do so. They have been fighting Turkey for decades. I held off this fight for almost three years, but it is time for us to get out of these ridiculous endless wars, many of them tribal, and bring our soldiers home. We will fight where it is to our benefit, and only fight to win."[75]

Trump's muscular language masked a stunning and demoralizing desertion of a loyal ally. In the same way, Obama's temporizing on his red line, his refusal to walk his own talk, masked a desertion of the Syrian rebels who had looked to the United States for support. Trump talks boldly about defending Ameri-

---

75 Johnson, Alex, Lederman, Josh, Smith, Marc, and Talmazan, Yuliya. "U.S. prepares to withdraw from northern Syria before Turkish operation," NBC News, 7 Oct. 2019, https://www.nbcnews.com/news/world/u-s-says-it-will-stand-aside-turkey-moves-syria-n1063106

can prerogatives in the Middle East, but his actions represent an abandonment of our responsibilities there—albeit in a different way, and with a different style, than Obama employed.

The Obama and Trump approaches have two points of commonality. First, they represent a conscious diminution of American influence in the Middle East, a willful retreat from generational leadership in this pivotal but troubled region of the world. Second, they both work primarily to the benefit of one man: Vladimir Putin.

Russia Ascendant

One American retreat after another in the Middle East has created a power vacuum that Putin stepped in to fill. He has played his hand brilliantly and seized on American weakness for years, and by now, he has established a position of strength and influence in the region that likely would never have been possible had successive American administrations been less willing to abdicate leadership. Russia is the Middle East's new power broker. Under Putin, Moscow has achieved a level of influence in the region that exceeds, arguably, that of the old Soviet Union.

How did he do it? With strategic cunning, with unshakable conviction about where Russian interests lay, and with keen recognition that his American rival did not want to play the game anymore. This recognition emboldened Putin in the knowledge that, if he acted firmly, he could establish new footholds for Russia that the Americans would not resist. His instinct in this regard has proved uncannily accurate.

Consider the case of Syria, the most dramatic setting for Putin's ascendance in the Middle East and the American retreat.

Back in 2011, during Obama's first term, the United States imposed an embargo against Damascus after Bashar al-Assad's government moved violently against protesters who opposed his regime—action that eventually initiated the Syrian Civil War. When an insurgency developed into the Syrian Democratic Forces, Washington backed the rebels, and it looked, for a time, as if Assad's days were numbered. Obama even called for the dictator to step down. Assad, it seemed, would be the latest dictator to be forced from office—and, in 2011, the year of the Arab Spring, his abdication would be, by far, the most dramatic victory for the forces of democracy.

What Washington and its allies did not count on was Vladimir Putin. The Russian leader backed Assad from the outset, standing up for him against the international outcry at the UN Security Council and crafting a disarmament agreement with which Syria agreed to comply—but with no attendant threat of military force if it did not. Putin made sure of that. Putin even suggested that it may have been the rebels, not the Assad regime, that had committed the chemical weapons attack. Even more importantly, Putin armed the Syrian dictator with whatever he needed to put down the insurgency—even as he cautioned the West against arming the rebels, claiming that doing so was a violation of international law.

There is no sign, as best I can determine, that U.S. intelligence or State Department officials had any appreciation or anticipation of how determinedly Putin was prepared to intervene in the Syrian conflict. Putin had already seen more than enough of the Arab Spring, and he was none too keen on American efforts in Libya, where another civil war was unfolding that would depose longtime dictator Muammar Gaddafi. Putin saw

Assad as salvageable—and it was important to save him, the Russian leader believed, to demonstrate that the United States and NATO could not simply intervene in every authoritarian country that they wished until they had secured democratic governments to their liking. Someone had to push back on Western interventionism, somewhere. Putin believed that he was the man, and that Syria was the place.

Of course, he had other goals in mind, too. He saw Syria as the staging ground for a reclamation of Russian influence in the Middle East, as well as a message to the Western powers that Russia was once again a force in international politics. "The idea," one Russian analyst put it, was "to use Syria as a bargaining chip in relations with the West."[76] Putin would save Assad, and in doing so, demonstrate Russian primacy.

The military, economic, and diplomatic support that Russia provided indeed saved the Assad regime. In the face of a determined Western effort, the Russian-backed Syrian military turned the tide against the rebels. Though world opinion lamented a conflict grisly in its human costs and blamed Assad for much of it, the Syrian strongman held on and prevailed. Today, he remains in power, more secure than he has been in years. Without Putin, Assad would be long gone from Syria—and probably dead.

It's hard to find any area in which Russia did not achieve its goals in Syria. In saving Assad, Putin established the Russian military's footprint in Syria, and in the Middle East, in a way

---

76   Charap, Samuel, Treyger, Elina, and Geist, Edward. "Understanding Russia's Intervention in Syria." Rand Corporation, 2019, https://www.rand.org/pubs/research_reports/RR3180.html

few American observers had contemplated. Before the Syrian Civil War, the American military presence in the Middle East was essentially unchecked; now, America faces serious limitations on its options and maneuverability. The Russians have moved in, and they aren't leaving.

By establishing himself as a player, Putin also established Russia as a diplomatic and negotiating force in the Middle East. Boots on the ground tend to do that, a lesson that Washington planners seem to have forgotten. So influential a hand did Russia wield that the ceasefire agreement, recognized internationally, was essentially negotiated on Putin's terms—not those of the West.

And, though he was careful, rhetorically, not to seem as if he condoned ethnic cleansing, Putin's backing of Assad allowed the dictator to do just that in Syria—which helped create Europe's Syrian refugee crisis, and which, in turn, helped destabilize and delegitimize the European Union, with its attendant effects, from rising right-wing nationalist parties to Brexit. Europe, especially Germany, is stuck with these huge influxes of refugees for as long as Assad remains in power in Syria—and that's looking to be a long time indeed.

Under Trump, the United States is simply walking away from these challenges. When Trump pulled American troops from northern Syria, it gave Turkey free rein to move against the Kurdish forces there, which Ankara has long wanted to suppress. And this, too, plays into Assad's hands—and Putin's—since it gives the emboldened Syrian government fresh opportunity to retake control over these areas. Putin knows that the U.S. will not challenge the deepening alliance between Moscow and Damascus, which has now expanded to include the first joint naval exercises in the Mediterranean, off the coast of Tartus, home to Russia's only naval base outside the territory of the former Soviet Union. Assad has vowed that he will regain mastery of all of Syria, and Russia is determined to help him do it. Now Trump is helping, too.

"Vladimir Putin is now the indispensable strategic arbiter in Syria," writes Jonathan Spyer in the *Wall Street Journal*. "None of the remaining pieces on the broken chessboard can move without Mr. Putin's hand... Mr. Assad, the Kurds, Turkey and Israel all now depend on Moscow's approval to advance their interests in Syria... All roads to Syria now run through Moscow. Mr. Putin could hardly ask for more."

It's hard to avoid the conclusion that Putin has become the prime mover in the Middle East, especially when one considers the trajectory of Russia's relationship with Turkey—a NATO member once firmly in the orbit of the United States. Admittedly, the Moscow-Ankara relationship has proved highly volatile in recent years, even recent months, and the likelihood that it will remain so for the time being is high. But what's striking is how, even through some periods of intense conflict, the two nations continue to try to work through their differences, in ways that that they had not shown inclination to do before. As recently as 2015, for example, diplomatic relations between Turkey and Russia were on the skids, after the Turks shot down a Russian fighter jet along the Syrian border. But Putin and Turkish president Recep Tayyip Erdoğan persevered through that tense period, and Erdoğan clearly began seeing his interests better served in Moscow. Infuriating the U.S. and its NATO partners, Erdoğan agreed to purchase Russia's $2.5 billion S-400 missile-defense system. Seeing that transaction as a breach of

NATO security, the U.S. canceled a deal to supply Turkey with F-35 fighters.

With the Americans out of the Syrian picture, Putin and Erdoğan have worked together in dividing up sectors of influence in the country, drawing up a joint agreement that represents a clear change in control in northern Syria. And Putin and Erdoğan have inaugurated a dual natural gas line, TurkStream, that will connect their countries, representing a new path for Russian gas exports into Turkey—and Europe. Erdoğan hailed the agreement as a demonstration of Turkey and Russia's "win-win cooperation."[77]

More recently, tensions have begun surfacing in the relationship again—and as noted, they will continue. Russia and Turkey will never be natural or easy partners. Nonetheless, it's a remarkable trajectory, and it couldn't have happened without American acquiescence and the collective loss of will of U.S. policymakers.

Putin's Shadow

The shadow of Putin's influence is spreading across the Middle East.

In Libya, Russia is working behind the scenes to attempt to install an autocratic leader in a country whose previous strongman, Gaddafi, was deposed with the help of the United States in 2011. Many point to these events as crucial in motivating Putin's intervention in Syria. As a staunch defender of authoritarian,

---

77   Bilginsoy, Zeynep. "Erdogan, Putin launch new gas line, vow Mideast diplomacy," AP, 8 Jan. 2020, https://apnews.com/a9b4a850252 I be3b3accc7be302913ab

anti-democratic systems, Putin had seen the United States and the Western powers eliminate two of the world's most notorious strongmen—Saddam Hussein and Gaddafi—in the span of a decade. According to former Kremlin adviser Sergei Markov, Putin believed that the U.S. was actually intent on destabilizing the Middle East, and he was determined to prevent the Americans from engineering the overthrow of other authoritarian leaders in the region.[78] Those who puzzle over Putin's actions in Syria generally fail to understand this context.

In Libya, where chaos has reigned since Gaddafi's fall, Putin sees a chance to reinstate an older order. Putin is backing Libyan strongman Field Marshal Khalifa Haftar, Commander of the Libyan National Army, in the current civil war. Russian mercenaries have fought alongside Haftar's troops in Tripoli. Putin's effort represents yet another challenge to waning American power in the region. He can strike, again, at the established international order that America and its Western allies had long considered sacrosanct—namely, the trend toward democratic leadership in countries around the world. Putin sees dictatorships as preferable to the Western alliance systems that overthrew autocratic leaders, and in Libya, as in Syria earlier, he sees the opportunity to advance his principles. The American Enterprise Institute's Emily Estelle emphasizes how American weakness enables Putin's efforts:

---

78 Weir, Fred. "Russia Worried About a Nuclear Iran. Russia worried about a nuclear Iran, but leery of US sanctions." *Christian Science Monitor*, 11 Jan. 2012, https://www.csmonitor.com/World/Europe/2012/0111/Russia-worried-about-a-nuclear-Iran-but-leery-of-US-sanctions

Mr. Putin wants to put a new Gadhafi in power to show that revolutions are doomed to fail and that he, not the U.S. or NATO, is an effective power broker in the region.

Mr. Putin aims to undermine America's post-Cold War leadership of the international order by casting the West as hypocritical and building an alliance system of like-minded autocrats... The U.S. has only worsened the situation by appearing to be an unreliable ally—to the Kurds in Syria and to the Libyan forces who fought ISIS with U.S. support but now face Mr. Haftar's airstrikes.[79]

Putin has also become a player in Afghanistan, another country where American influence is waning. Over the last several years, the Russian president has forged closer ties with the Taliban, with whom he has played an increasingly active role in the country's ongoing civil war. For Russia, getting closer to the Taliban became essential after the rise of ISIS, whom Putin viewed as a direct threat to Russian interests. Some reports suggest that Russia may have begun providing military assistance to the Taliban. And in June 2020, American intelligence officials announced that they had uncovered evidence that Russia was paying Taliban militants to kill U.S. troops in Afghanistan. President Trump's refusal even to acknowledge the reality that Russia has been targeting American troops represents a sickening dereliction of presidential leadership and underscores, again, the abandonment of American authority in the Middle East.

---

79   Estelle, Emily. "Don't Let Russia Dominate Libya." Wall Street Journal, 2 Dec. 2019, https://www.wsj.com/articles/dont-let-russia-dominate-libya-11575330409

Russia's relatively modest effort—so far—in Afghanistan contrasts with a much more vigorous role in Yemen, where an ongoing civil war has become nearly as destabilizing in recent years as the Syrian situation. Raging since 2015, the civil war pits two factions: the Yemeni government in exile, headed by Mansur Hadi, and the Houthi rebels, both of which claim to be the country's legitimate governing force. The Houthis forced Hadi to flee the country in 2014, but the following year, the war began in earnest, as Saudi Arabia and other nations—including the U.S.—began bombing the Houthi rebels in an attempt to restore Hadi's government.

The largely Shia Houthi rebels are supported by Iran, which has sent the rebels weaponry—including improvised explosive devices (IEDs), explosively formed penetrators (EFPs), and unmanned aerial vehicles (UAVs)—and military advisors in a conflict that shapes up along familiar Sunni-Shia lines and has implications for the broader region. Tehran has provided training to Houthi fighters; given the Houthis access to its missile capabilities; and has itself directed some of the Houthis' missile attacks against Saudi Arabia. The arms seized from Houthi fighters by the Saudi-led coalition have been identified as Iran-made. In short, the Houthis owe what military prowess they possess to Iran.

And Iran owes its ability to supply the Houthis to Russia. While much focus in the Yemeni conflict remains, understandably, on the proxy war being fought between Saudi Arabia, on the government's side, and Iran, on the Houthi rebels' side, the role that Russia has played is often overlooked. Iran's role in the conflict is largely coordinated with Moscow. Writing about the conflict for the Jerusalem Institute for Strategy and Security,

Micky Aharonson and Yossi Mansharof maintain that "Iranian activity depends on cooperation with Russia, which protects [Iran] against unfavorable Security Council resolutions and enables [it] to continue exporting terrorism to Yemen. Russia is therefore an important actor enabling Iran to extend its hold and influence in Yemen. Among other things, Russia makes it possible for Iran to foster the deadly terrorist attacks committed by the Houthis in Yemen and their missile barrages aimed at Saudi Arabia."[80] The Houthis seem to understand this as well: Houthi delegations have met with the Russian deputy foreign minister and have declared that Moscow should be integral to any negotiated settlement in Yemen. Again, through vigorous action and intervention, Putin has enlarged Russia's influence.

Russia's working in concert with Iran in countries like Syria and Yemen makes clear just how integral the Tehran-Moscow partnership is to Putin's broader Middle East strategy. Though the two countries continue to have important differences, their strategic cooperation shows no sign of diminishing. They are, in matters of practical fact, allies on most important issues—and the overarching point of unity is their mutual determination to oppose the West, especially the United States. Russian-Iranian military ties continue to deepen, as shown by a 2019 agreement between the Russian Defense Ministry and the Iranian Armed Forces calling for expanding military cooperation between the two countries. And the entire experience in Syria, over nearly a decade now, in which Russia and Iran have stood by one an-

---

80   Aharonson, Micky, and Mansharof, Yossi. "Iranian-Russian Cooperation in Yemen." Jerusalem Institute for Strategy and Security, 1 Mar. 2019, https://jiss.org.il/en/aharonson-mansharof-iranian-russian-cooperation-in-yemen/

other—and by Bashar al-Assad—has unquestionably forged a stronger partnership.

The Russia-Iran relationship was newly tested by Trump's killing of Soleimani, but Putin and Iranian president Rouhani quickly made clear that the two nations intended to stick close together. Of course, the American move was an audacious one, with potentially dramatic consequences. From Putin's perspective, the concern was to ensure that it did not alter the new realities on the ground that he had worked so hard to secure. Iran shared that goal; neither country wanted to see the Soleimani killing degrading Hezbollah's capabilities, for instance, or affecting developments in Syria, which were going their way. Still respecting American hard power, though, Putin was careful not to make any suggestion of support for major Iranian retaliation. What he wanted most of all was calm, and a dialing down of tensions between Washington and Tehran.

For the time being, he has gotten that. Tehran launched a half-hearted missile attack on an American base in Iraq a few days later that caused no casualties; it was a face-saving measure. As long as no major new crisis was in the offing, Putin could pursue his long-term goals of expanding Russia's Middle East influence, often at American expense. The Soleimani killing, dramatic as it was, didn't change that calculus.

And, I submit, it won't change it—because in the end, Putin comes out ahead from this episode, too.

Consider how the Soleimani strike divided the Americans against their allies, not only in Western Europe but also in the Middle East. Infuriated by violation of its sovereignty in an attack that it was not warned about, Iraq's parliament held a ceremonial vote in favor of asking American troops to leave the country. The vote was a political gesture, and not binding, but it dramatized how Trump's decision was driving a wedge between the U.S. and its partners—and Putin was only too happy to expand that divide. If the U.S. does indeed go on to withdraw its troops from Iraq, it will have little or no leverage in influencing events in Syria—another win for Putin.

More broadly, post-Soleimani, Russia stands to gain from America's increasingly erratic behavior in the region. As noted above, Putin had already changed the strategic dynamic between the United States and Turkey, moving in to foster closer relations with Erdoğan after Trump announced the U.S. withdrawal from Syria. In the wake of the Soleimani killing, Turkey, sounding very much like a Moscow ally, released a statement condemning "foreign interventions, assassinations and sectarian conflicts in the region." Once the Middle East's strong hand, the United States has become an unpredictable actor. Putin, by contrast, looks like a rock of stability. All the region's players know where he stands.

The truth is plain: Trump's boasts notwithstanding, the biggest winner of the Soleimani episode is not the United States or Donald Trump, but Russia and Vladimir Putin. Trump apologists focus on the death of Soleimani and the (likely temporary) damage to the Iranian military apparatus, but they neglect to acknowledge, again, how the strike actually weakens the United States in important ways—for example, by further damaging our European alliances. Trump apparently didn't even give the British the courtesy of a heads' up about the strike. Europe has opposed Trump's withdrawal from the nuclear deal with Iran— as did Putin, who criticized the American decision vigorously. The Soleimani strike may yet wind up resulting in Iran's total abandonment of the agreement—it has already announced that it will stop honoring some of its restrictions—which could lead to it getting a nuclear weapon sooner. If that happens, one can readily imagine the bitterness on the European side at what will surely be seen as another instance of cowboy-like American recklessness.

And if that dark day comes, who will be able to say that he had worked hard with Europe to prevent it, to keep the Iranians in the agreement? Putin. And who will be there to pick up the pieces if such a development opens further fissures in relations between American and its Western European allies? Putin, again. The Russian president has labored for years to erode Western alliances, and he continues to make headway toward that goal, independent of the Soleimani episode. French president Emanuel Macron is seeking better relations with Moscow. German prime minister Angela Merkel is working closely with Putin on the Nordstream 2 pipeline that will bring natural gas into the European Union—and bypass Ukraine. With or without Middle East tensions, Europe is moving closer into Putin's orbit. Erratic American behavior, ranging from dramatic provocations to sudden withdrawals, is likely to move it closer still.

It's Russia's Middle East Now

Vladimir Putin is now the Middle East's powerbroker. His ascent in the region represents a remarkable transformation of geopolitics, engineered by a man who leads a country with major liabilities and weaknesses but who has played his hand with skill, guile, and ruthlessness. It is Putin who speaks the language of the Middle East—namely, power politics, the politics of autocratic rule and strongmen tactics. It is a region long run by such rulers, and the United States, with its tireless efforts to promote democracy and regime change and supposedly "universal" Western values, has always been at odds with it. Yet, up until recently, most countries in the region had to deal, one way or another, with the Americans. Putin's emergence has changed that dynamic, and, more recently, so has Donald Trump's evidently sincere desire to disengage the U.S. from the thankless role of peacemaker and broker in the region.

Trump won the presidency in no small part by promising an end to "endless wars," by which he meant, unmistakably, the wars that the U.S. had been fighting in the Middle East. He also stressed—refreshingly, to some degree—the importance of considering the national interest in making decisions about such commitments. Trump was surely correct in pointing to the excesses and overreach of the liberal internationalist view of American foreign policy, a view that transcended party identification and encompassed the mainstream of both the Republican and Democratic parties. So, to a limited extent, Trump's critique and even some of his walk-back has been constructive.

The problem is twofold: first, Trump has gone too far with his plans for disengagement. As the pullback from Syria makes painfully clear, Putin will fill that vacuum eagerly, to say nothing of the lamentable precedent that Trump has set by deserting longstanding allies in a dangerous part of the world. Second, Trump's neo-isolationist policy couldn't come at a worse time—just at the point when Putin had already been making nearly a decade's worth of headway in the Middle East, exploiting the mistakes and overcommitments of the United States in Iraq and Afghanistan to pursue a new role in the region. Trump's retreat, taken in tandem with Putin's long-pursued agenda of power expansion, will prove a devastating combination for the Middle East—and for the world. Like other Putin triumphs, it could not have happened without American acquiescence.

CHAPTER FIVE

The Military and Nuclear Picture

I NDIVIDUALLY AND COLLECTIVELY, RUSSIA AND CHINA ARE building up their military capacities and have been doing so for years. During the Obama administration, these efforts went largely unaddressed in terms of a committed U.S. policy response. The Trump administration, via its published National Security Strategy, has at least made clear that it recognizes the challenges a budding Russia-China military axis poses. What it will do about it remains to be seen.

Russia has been actively rebuilding its military for more than a decade—bolstering ground forces, upgrading air and missile defenses, enhancing drone and cyber capabilities, and shoring up special operations units. Overall, Moscow increased military spending 87 percent between 2007 and 2016.[81] Currently, Russian ground troops number about 350,000.

---

81 South, Todd. "What's Putin up to? The Russian military buildup in Europe raises tension." Military Times, 13 Sep. 2017, https://www.militarytimes.com/news/2017/09/13/whats-putin-up-to-the-russian-military-buildup-on-europes-border-raises-tension/

Russian air defenses, according to *Military Times*, can "hold NATO airpower at bay while rockets and artillery, alongside drone-focused ISR, can target U.S. and NATO forces."[82] Moscow seems ever-more determined to test NATO capabilities and resolve.

This is most evident in Moscow's continued incursions and buildup in Kaliningrad, a disconnected Russian territory, or "exclave," between Lithuania and Poland on the Baltic Sea widely regarded as Moscow's "strategic outpost" on the border of NATO territory. Russia appears to be working on upgrades to four of its military installations in Kaliningrad and on a nuclear-weapons storage site there, along with construction of dozens of new bunkers near Primorsk, a Baltic Sea port. The Russians delivered nuclear-capable Iskander missiles to their base in Chernyakhovsk, in Kaliningrad, in February 2019.[83]

"If they want to challenge us, we will challenge them," says Admiral James G. Foggo III, commander of U.S. Naval Forces Europe-Africa and the Allied Joint Force Command in Naples. "We're not going to be intimidated by those systems that are out there."[84] But Kaliningrad surely stands as a Russian challenge to the West.

---

82   South, Todd. "What's Putin up to? The Russian military buildup in Europe raises tension." Military Times, 13 Sep. 2017, https://www.militarytimes.com/news/2017/09/13/whats-putin-up-to-the-russian-military-buildup-on-europes-border-raises-tension/

83   Pickrell, Ryan. "New photos show Russia's building up its military on NATO's doorstep, but the alliance says it won't be intimidated." Business Insider, 18 Oct. 2018, https://www.businessinsider.com/it-looks-like-russias-building-up-its-military-on-natos-doorstep-2018-10.

84   Liebermann, Oren, Pleitgen, Frederik, and Cotovio, Vasco.
"New satellite images suggest military buildup in Russia's strategic Baltic enclave." CNN, 17 Oct. 2018, https://www.cnn.com/2018/10/17/europe/russia-kaliningrad-military-buildup-intl/index.html

Of greatest concern remains Russia's ongoing menacing of Ukraine. Ever since 2014, when Russia annexed Crimea, a peninsula south of Ukraine, tensions have been high in the region, not only between Moscow and Kiev but also between Russia and the United States. Moscow says that it has no plans to return Crimea to Ukraine, despite U.S. and Western demands that it do so, and the focus in the West has shifted from reclaiming Crimea to thwarting new Putin aggressions.

Those might be in the offing, in any case. Ukraine officials have warned the United States and its allies of a major Russian buildup in the country—troops, tanks, and artillery—that they suggest could be preparatory to an invasion. Former Ukraine president Petro Poroshenko said that Moscow has 80,000 troops on the border; national officials cite satellite images showing "rows of tanks and armored personnel carriers at two sites in southern Russia, and military transport planes parked at an air base in Crimea," according to a December 2018 report in the *New York Times*.[85] The Russians themselves boasted about deployment of S-400 antiaircraft missiles at the airbase. As for the tanks, they're stationed at a depot near a portion of the Ukrainian border controlled by pro-Moscow separatists. U.S. intelligence official, speaking on background, told technology journalist Patrick Tucker that Russia was conducting "a deliberate and systematic buildup of their forces" on the Crimean Peninsula. It's not clear how much of this is new or significant, but Ukrainians are worried. "Here we see a concentration of

---

85   Kramer, Andrew E. "Ukraine Asserts Major Russian Military Buildup on Eastern Border." New York Times, 15 Dec. 2018, https://www.nytimes.com/2018/12/15/world/europe/ukraine-russia-military-buildup.html.

Russian armaments on our border, not some regular drills," said Volodymyr V. Fesenko, director of a political studies institute in Kiev. The Ukrainians also say that Russia is upgrading facilities in Crimea to store nuclear weapons.

All told, the buildup makes clear that Russia has no intention of returning Crimea to Ukrainian possession, an action that the United States continues to insist on, at least officially. It's hard to believe that the U.S. really thinks anything like that is possible, at this point, anyway, especially since Moscow likely has other strategic goals in mind—like gaining more control over the Black Sea, "which then affords them the ability to project power beyond their immediate environment," says Sarah Bidgood, director of the Eurasia Nonproliferation Program at the James Martin Center for Nonproliferation Studies. The Russians are arming up in the Black Sea, adding ten warships that can deliver the Kalibr cruise missile (which can hit targets up to 1,500 miles away), six diesel-electric Kilo-class attack submarines, and four surface ships. "This is a significant buildup," says Bidgood. "NATO is going to be under increasing pressure from allies in the region to show that it's able to push back against Russian attempts to gain greater control of the Black Sea. To me, that's a really dangerous environment."[86]

Further support for that interpretation comes from an unnamed U.S. intelligence officer, who told Defense One that, in his view, Russia's Black Sea buildup has aims that extend well be-

---

86 Tucker, Patrick. "US Intelligence Officials and Satellite Photos Detail Russian Military Buildup on Crimea." Defense One, 12 June 2019, https://www.defenseone.com/threats/2019/06/exclusive-satellite-photos-detail-russian-military-buildup-crimea/157642/

yond the Black Sea. "A lot of the stuff for their operations in Syria was coming out of the Black Sea, so we would see a heightened [operational] tempo as a result for that... Any time it becomes apparent we might strike into Syria as a response for chemical weapons use or something like that, you'll see ships coming out of the Black Sea, moving down into the Mediterranean." Retired Lieutenant General Ben Hodges, who served as commander of the U.S. Army Europe, agrees. The Black Sea, he says, is Russia's "launching pad into the Middle East and Eastern Mediterranean. It's essential for their resupply into Syria, [which] has to come through the Black Sea, through the Dardanelles."[87]

What the Russians are doing here represents another instance of what might be called fait accompli logic. A major and operations officer for the U.S. Army's First Battalion authored a report expressing skepticism about the American military's ability to dislodge the Russians from certain pieces of Eastern Europe, if the Russians were to pursue further aggression. While the report argued that American and NATO forces could hold off Russia from a broader offensive, its concern was that the Western allies would bring inadequate, and tardy, forces to bear on Russian incursions into areas closer to Ukraine or Crimea— what Russia calls its "near abroad." Russian forces would simply be too entrenched to dislodge. And that's really the point.

The report's author, Major Amos C. Fox, points out how battle-hardened Russian forces in the region have become and how their combat seasoning outstrips that of most American troops. The Russians have fought "significant battles and waged deci-

---

87 Ibid.

sive sieges on a scale that vastly exceeds what the U.S. Army brigade combat teams (BCTs) can experience at combat training centers… These battles are important because they remind students of war that rugged, land-centric combined arms warfare has not been thrown into the dustbin of history but is instead alive and well," he writes.[88] Hodges is impressed by the Russians' speed of logistical coordination in Eastern Europe, which he believes is superior to NATO's, in part because "Russia faces no international boundaries or customs procedures that could inhibit movement in a crisis."[89]

The Russians are well-equipped in the region, with generous supplies of tanks, armored personnel carriers, and artillery pieces to multiple-launch rocket systems. And their forces are adept at the asymmetrical warfare that Russia has wielded so skillfully in recent years, from misinformation campaigns and social media recruiting of proxy fighters. All told, Russia presents a formidable force in the region—and a daunting adversary for American forces, should direct conflict arise. "The fact that Russia has rotated 27 brigades and regiments through the Donbas while the U.S. Army possesses only 31 BCTs must not be overlooked," writes Fox. "The Russian military, especially its ground forces and its combat experience, need to be respected."[90]

---

88 South, Todd. "Russian military gains in Ukraine could spell trouble for the US Army, even in a conventional fight." Army Times, 14 May 2019,
https://www.armytimes.com/news/your-army/2019/05/14/russian-military-gains-in-ukraine-could-spell-trouble-for-the-us-army-even-in-a-conventional-fight/

89 Ibid.

90 Ibid.

This sentiment goes double for the military experience that the Russians have gained during the Syrian conflict, where Russian success in saving Assad—and, in the process, becoming the Middle East's new power broker—have reversed older, unhappy memories of intervention in that region, such as Moscow's Afghanistan debacle of the 1980s. Russian success in Syria has also boosted confidence in the nation's current state of military effectiveness—a major improvement from a decade ago, when the Russian war in Georgia revealed embarrassing shortcomings in military capabilities. Much has changed since then. The Russian military has reinvigorated itself, both materially and morally.

And the Russian nuclear force is undergoing a similar upgrade. Putin is developing a host of new strategic nuclear weapons to counter what he sees as American provocations in developing a global missile-defense system. Putin sees this as an American attempt to undermine Russia's nuclear deterrent, and so he has set off on a determined path to develop a class of weapons that neutralize this advantage.

These include a new class of missiles designed to bypass American missile-defense systems. Russia's Sarmat ICBM is the key player here. Its range exceeds that of previous Russian systems, and its shorter boost phase gives missile-defense systems less time to detect it. But its most troubling capability is that its flight path can cover the South Pole, thus evading current American missile-defense capabilities. Putin acknowledges this bluntly: the Sarmat, he says, "can attack targets both via the North and South poles. Sarmat is a formidable missile and, owing to its characteristics, is untroubled by even the most advanced missile defense systems."[91] Russia is also developing a nuclear-powered cruise missile. Putin, whose enthusiasm for these weapons is evident in his extensive public descriptions of them, describes it as "a low-flying stealth missile carrying a nuclear warhead, with almost an unlimited range, unpredictable trajectory and ability to bypass interception boundaries." He boasts that it is "is invincible against all existing and prospective missile defense and counter-air defense systems."[92]

It really is striking to hear the Russian president wax so enthusiastically about his nation's new generation of nuclear hardware. Here he is, talking about the intercontinental-range nuclear torpedo, an underwater vehicle that would carry a 100-megaton warhead:

> We have developed unmanned submersible vehicles that can move at great depths—I would say extreme depths—intercontinentally, at a speed multiple times higher than the speed of submarines, cutting-edge torpedoes and all kinds of surface vessels, including some of the fastest. It is really fantastic. They are quiet, highly maneuverable and have hardly any vulnerabilities for the enemy to exploit. There is simply nothing in the world capable of withstanding them. Unmanned underwater vehicles can carry either conventional or nuclear warheads, which enables them to engage various targets, including aircraft groups, coastal fortifications and infrastructure.[93]

------

91   Majumdar, Dave. "Russia's Nuclear Weapons Buildup Is Aimed at Beating U.S. Missile Defenses." The National Interest, 1 Mar. 2018, https://nationalinterest.org/blog/the-buzz/russias-nuclear-weapons-buildup-aimed-beating-us-missile-24716

92   Ibid.

93   Ibid.

Even allowing for bluster and overstatement, most Russian military experts agree that what Putin has described is largely accurate. "Most of this is reality, it's just a question of near or distant reality," says Michael Kofman of the Center for Naval Analyses, a specialist in Russian military affairs.[94] The programs are real, he says—and plausible.

What's most concerning about the Russian nuclear efforts is twofold. First, some of these new weapons would fall outside of the current U.S.-Russia New START agreement, negotiated by the Obama administration, and, though highly imperfect (as I've written previously), one of the few remaining agreements curtailing nukes between the two superpowers, with the U.S. exit from the IMF Treaty at Trump's direction, and, earlier, under George W. Bush, its exit from the ABM Treaty. Second, and even more worrisome, is the emergency of "hypersonic" nuclear weapons—nukes that can travel at multiples of the speed of sound, arriving at their targets in a matter of minutes, leaving leaders in targeted countries an incredibly compressed amount of time in which to decide on a response. The advent of hypersonic weaponry will surely usher in a new age of nuclear anxiety and perhaps nuclear blackmail. Future arms agreements between the U.S. and Russia, if there are any, must reckon with these weapons. In the meantime, Putin is determined to arm up.

China Arms Up

Meantime, in Beijing, another military buildup proceeds, under the leadership of Xi Jinping, who has styled himself as the mod-

------

94   Ibid.

ern savior of the People's Liberation Army—and, by extension, of China itself. Consider the opening images of the Chinese documentary, *Strong Military*, which shows Xi standing aboard the guided missile destroyer *Haikou*, which sails into the South China as Xi looks out through binoculars. A voiceover intones: "As the warship pierces the waves, Xi Jinping peers toward a vision obscured in the mist of history when, 170 years ago, Western powers came from the sea to open the door to China, beginning a bitter nightmare for ancient China"—a period of imperial subjugation regarded with shame in China. Only with the Communist victory in 1948 does that nightmare end, according to the film, and the leadership of men like Mao and Deng Xiaoping. The film clearly positions Xi as the next great figure in this lineage, with a vision as mighty as those of his predecessors.

Indeed, Xi's ambitions are Mao-like in their grandiosity, and this is particularly evident in his extensive efforts to overhaul and remake the People's Liberation Army, 2 million strong. He is a unique and formidable leader for the PLA at this point in Chinese history. His identification with the army is so strong that he has taken to wearing camouflage fatigues and combat boots when he reviews military parades. and China under Xi has staged some of its largest military parades since the Communist Revolution.

"Xi Jinping is obsessed with military parades," says Willy Lam Wo-lap, professor at the Chinese University of Hong Kong. "He loves these demonstrations of raw power." And he likes to make clear that authority begins and ends with him. Sometimes he has occupied the reviewing stand alone, without the usual assortment of other Communist officials, and he makes sure that commanders and generals salute him. There is no ambiguity about where authority lies.

In the process of overhauling a vast military bureaucracy and initiating an intense purge of corruption, Xi has placed himself at the head of the chain of military command. He has shown a willingness to make radical changes.

"When I talk to my mainland friends, they all say he is a risk taker," says Taiwan's former defense minister, Andrew Yang. "You never know what his next move will be."

The military overhaul has shown this insight to be true. Xi has turned the PLA's administration upside down, cutting 300,000 non-combat personnel in 2015, dramatically reorganizing regional structures and commands, and elevating new figures to leadership positions. All these efforts share common themes—they have made the PLS more streamlined in its organizational structure, and they have ensured that all paths of accountability trace back directly to Xi himself. Some observers believe that these efforts reflect an internal power struggle within the Party and the military; if so, Xi has clearly won it.

Another aspect of the overhaul is the anti-corruption push, waged against a long-entrenched bureaucracy that had settled into a culture of self-dealing. Xi has purged more than 100 generals from the ranks, for causes ranging from corruption to disloyalty. He recognizes no distinctions of service or seniority in doing so. The most senior officer convicted in his purge, former general Guo Boxiong, was made to confess, on state television, to bribery charges. "The Central Military Commission dealt with my case completely correctly," Guo said to the cameras. "I must confess my guilt and take responsibility for it." If he was expecting leniency for his admission, though, he was disappointed. He is now serving a life sentence.

All this change is being put toward the goal of making the PLA into a far more offensively capable force than it has historically been. The People's Liberation Army is busy producing aircraft carriers, stealth bombers, amphibious troop carriers, and other hardware, all part of a growing military budget that Xi has given senior military officers major roles in formulating. China wants to build a naval and missile force that will rival any in the world. Currently, Beijing's navy includes 27 destroyers, 59 frigates, and 41 corvettes, totaling 127 surface ships, while as noted in Chapter 2, China has 45-50 modern submarines; all told, China's warships and subs total about 400.[95]

The Chinese navy currently has more ships than "Germany, India, Spain, and the United Kingdom combined," in the assessment of the Center for Strategic and International Studies.[96]

The focal point now, as it has been for years, is Beijing's aggression in the South China Sea. China has been constructing islands across this vast expanse for nearly a decade now, populating them with landing strips, military bases, and other military assets. It has expanded its bases, detection systems, and weapons-delivery systems, in the process antagonizing neighbors such as the Philippines and Vietnam, and causing tensions

---

95   Lague, David, and Kang Lim, Benjamin. "China's vast fleet is tipping the balance in the Pacific." Reuters, 30 Apr. 2019, https://www.reuters.com/investigates/special-report/china-army-navy/.

96   Mizokami, Kyle. "China Now Has More Warships Than the U.S." Popular Mechanics, 20 May 2019, https://www.popularmechanics.com/military/navy-ships/a27532437/china-now-has-more-warships-than-the-us/#:~:text=According%20to%20CSIS%2C%20the%20Chinese,and%20the%20United%20Kingdom%E2%80%9D%20combined.&text=The%20bulk%20of%20Beijing's%20Navy,total%20of%20119%20surface%20ships.

as well with the United States, viewed by many of these nations as their protector in the Pacific. It has placed long-range surface-to-air missiles and anti-ship cruise missiles on the disputed Spratly Islands, even as Xi claims that China has no plans to militarize these sea lanes. The incursions continue.

Patrick Shanahan, then serving as President Trump's acting defense secretary, deemed these moves "excessive" and "overkill," but Beijing has not backed down.[97] "Building facilities on one's own territories is not militarization," said Lieutenant General Wei Fenghe.[98] China claims that its construction of military installations has to do with civilian and rescue operations, though the intensity of military assets in evidence makes this explanation hard to accept.

On the nuclear side, while China's nuclear arsenal remains modest compared with those of Russia and the United States, Beijing is clearly ramping up efforts to build out this capability. To some extent, China's laggard status, until recently, has to do with a different way of thinking about nukes. The Chinese Communists generally regarded nukes as a defensive last resort, and thus pursued technological advances solely on the basis of maintaining rough parity with the U.S. and Russia—not on competing with their arsenals as a serious offensive choice. The PLA's massive supply of manpower no doubt had much to

---

97 "Chinese militarization of South China Sea 'excessive': acting Pentagon chief." Reuters, 31 May 2019, https://www.reuters.com/article/us-asia-security-usa-china/chinese-militarization-of-south-china-sea-excessive-acting-pentagon-chief-idUSKCN1T118C

98 Roughneen, Simon. "China's Wei threatens 'fight to the end' with US." Asia Times, 2 June 2019, https://www.asiatimes.com/2019/06/article/chinas-wei-threatens-fight-to-the-end-with-us/.

do with this thinking. Now, however, under Xi, the Chinese are making some more aggressive efforts. The Pentagon warned in a 2019 report that the Chinese military was moving toward achievement of a nuclear triad—that is, capability of using nuclear weapons from land, air, and sea, as the U.S. and Russia are able to do. The last piece in the puzzle was an air-launched ballistic missile, thought to be nearing completion.

Currently, China has approximately 90 ICBMs in its nuclear arsenal. In the air, as the Pentagon puts it in its report, the PLA is "upgrading its aircraft with two new air-launched ballistic missiles, one of which may include a nuclear payload." The Americans explained that the deployment of this weapon would, for the first time, "provide China with a viable nuclear 'triad' of delivery systems dispersed across land, sea, and air forces." And at sea, China currently has four ballistic-missile submarines, with more on the way.

Taken together, the Chinese military overhaul, reinvestment, and buildup represent a quantum increase in military hard power—to a degree never before seen in the Pacific. China's new ability to project force, both in terms of lethality and scale, in the Pacific, represent nothing less than the end of U.S. supremacy in the region. The world's largest navy; missile capabilities rapidly catching up with American defenses; and the capability to launch nuclear missiles from submarines all present a threat that the United States has simply not had to deal with before in Asia. And all of this occurs in the context of Beijing's ongoing expansion of its bases and outposts across the South China Sea.

As I noted in the Pacific chapter, it is heartening that the United States is finally recognizing the dimensions of this challenge and taking some steps—boosting defense spending, including on naval expansion and new weapons development—to address it, though as I've noted, it is awfully late in the day to get started. No one can say with unblinking confidence, anymore, that if the United States and China should find themselves in a clash in the Pacific, that the U.S. would prevail. Certainty went out of that scenario some time ago.

Moreover, it's not the only scenario to worry about. I've described above some of the efforts that Moscow and Beijing have been undertaking to strengthen their military postures and strategic positions, always to the detriment of the United States. These efforts become more formidable still when one recognizes how closely the two nations now work together. Indeed, at this point, Chinese and Russian military cooperation has all the hallmarks of a partnership.

A Formidable Partnership

Perhaps most concerning of all is the growing evidence that China and Russia are cooperating and collaborating militarily to an unprecedented extent.

It starts with some written agreements, which, while not stipulating a formal alliance, clearly facilitate military ties and even joint action. In 2001, the two nations signed a bilateral Treaty of Good Neighborliness and Friendly Cooperation, part of which notes that "when a situation arises in which one of the contracting parties deems that peace is being threatened and undermined or its security interests are involved or when it is confronted with the threat of aggression, the contracting parties shall immediately hold contacts and consultations in order to eliminate such threats." A joint statement between

Russia and China nearly two decades later, in 2018, pledged that the nations would "build up cooperation in all areas, and further build up strategic contacts and coordination between their armed forces, improve the existing mechanisms of military cooperation, expand interaction in the field of practical military and military-technical cooperation and jointly resist challenges to global and regional security."[99] Both statements suggest an understanding that goes beyond mere assurances of cooperation.

And the evidence grows clearer each year that Russia and China are tangibly, not just verbally, cooperating militarily. Their decade-old "Peace Mission" is a joint military exercise involving both air and ground forces; they conduct naval exercises, too, under the auspices of the Shanghai Security Cooperation Organization (SCO). In 2018, Russia conducted its largest military drill since the fall of the Soviet Union, called Vostok 2018, involving hundreds of thousands of Russian troops—and 3,500 Chinese personnel from the People's Liberation Army joined in. NATO leaders condemned the exercise, but Putin and Xi were unfazed. Russia had "trustworthy ties in political, security and defense spheres" with China, Putin said. The relationship between the two countries, Xi said, was "getting stronger all the time."[100]

---

99   Gady, Franz-Stefan. "Why the West Should Not Underestimate China-Russia Military Ties." EastWest Institute, 30 Jan. 2019, https://www.eastwest.ngo/idea/why-west-should-not-underestimate-china-russia-military-ties.

100   "Russia begins its largest ever military exercise with 300,000 soldiers." The Guardian, 11 Sept. 2018, https://www.theguardian.com/world/2018/sep/11/russia-largest-ever-military-exercise-300000-soldiers-china.

Arms sales and technology transfers are accelerating between the two. "Russian and Chinese officials have repeatedly stressed that military-technical cooperation constitutes the backbone of the China-Russia strategic partnership," writes Franz-Stefan Gady of the East-West Institute.[101] China was the first foreign buyer of Russia's most advanced surface-to-air missile system, the S-400, and Beijing may purchase Moscow's newest stealth fighter, the Sukhoi Su-57, which can fight in the air as well as hitting targets on land and sea. China builds its own military aircraft but is dependent on Russian-made engines for these planes.

"Moscow has supported Beijing's military ambitions by providing sophisticated weapons platforms to the People's Liberation Army," says Richard Weitz of the Hudson Institute. "These weapons transfers have bolstered China's air defense, anti-ship, and other critical capabilities in significant ways... they have enhanced the PLA's capability to threaten foreign navies and air forces in the waters and airspace near China."[102]

Moscow and Beijing have even begun making common cause in the Arctic, aided by a seemingly disinterested United States, which has allowed both countries to make incursions where a stronger American hand might have deterred them. In a 2019 meeting of the Arctic Council, a regional forum usually

101   Gady, Franz-Stefan. "Why the West Should Not Underestimate China-Russia Military Ties." EastWest Institute, 30 Jan. 2019, https://www.eastwest.ngo/idea/why-west-should-not-underestimate-china-russia-military-ties.

102   Kliegman, Aaron. "China, Russia Deepening Defense Partnership." Washington Free Beacon, 14 May 2019, https://freebeacon.com/national-security/report-china-russia-deepening-defense-partnership/.

devoted to issues involving scientific and environmental issues, Secretary of State Mike Pompeo blasted the Russians and Chinese for their Arctic activities—making clear that, at long last, the United States has noticed how aggressively the two nations are moving there. Indeed, the Arctic looks central to both Russia and China's future plans: Beijing, seeking greater economic growth, is deploying ice-breakers and other assets into the polar waters, while the Russians, who have been there much longer, are creating or upgrading military bases and bolstering other assets, including nuclear subs, as they seek to exploit the region's vast resources.

"We'll finish building infrastructure in 2019 to accommodate air defense radar units and aviation guidance points on the Sredny and Wrangel Islands, and on Cape Schmidt" in the Russian Arctic, said Russian Defense Minister Sergei Shoigu.[103] For their part, the Chinese see the Arctic as part of their Polar Silk Road initiative and are trying, in the words of the Pentagon, to fashion themselves into a "near-Arctic state."[104]

Add it all up—both nations' independent military buildups, their increasingly aggressive activity toward neighbors in their respective regions, their growing participation with one another in joint military exercises, their deepening commitment in terms of signed agreements and arms sales, and their mutual interest in geographic areas of deep interest to the Unit-

---

103   "Russia says will build up Arctic military presence." France 24, 18 Dec. 2018, https://www.france24.com/en/20181218-russia-says-will-build-arctic-military-presence.

104   Capaccio, Anthony. "China Military Expanding Reach Into Arctic Region, Pentagon Says." Bloomberg, 2 May 2019, https://www.bloomberg.com/news/articles/2019-05-03/china-military-expanding-reach-into-arctic-region-pentagon-says.

ed States—and the military threat posed by the budding Russia-China alliance looks formidable indeed.

How formidable? "The U.S. could lose," says retired admiral Gary Roughead, former Chief of Naval Operations, the top post in the U.S. Navy. "We really are at a significant inflection point in history."[105] Roughead chaired a bipartisan committee evaluating the Trump administration's defense strategy, and its conclusion is stark. The committee sees the U.S. facing a "national security crisis," one stemming primarily from the growing military power of Russia and China. "U.S. military superiority is no longer assured and the implications for American interests and American security are severe."[106]

I drew the same conclusion years ago in *The Russia-China Axis*. It is even more relevant today.

We Need Allies

Clearly, the United States has its work cut out for it in addressing the Russia/China military challenge, a key component of which will involve updating the American military posture, both strategically and materially. In this regard, the U.S.-led NATO training exercises in Eastern Europe, known as Defender 2020, promised to be an event of considerable importance

---

105 "How China Is Replacing America as Asia's Military Titan." Haaretz, 23 Apr. 2019, https://www.haaretz.com/us-news/how-china-is-replacing-america-as-asia-s-military-titan-1.7160808.

106 Mehta, Aaron. "A 'crisis of national security': New report to Congress sounds alarm." Defense News, 14 Nov. 2018, https://www.defensenews.com/pentagon/2018/11/14/a-crisis-of-national-security-new-report-to-congress-sounds-alarm/.

for gauging preparedness and refining strategies. The exercises planned were to be the largest of their kind in 25 years; alas, the Army was forced to postpone them due to the coronavirus. It's not likely that they would be rescheduled before 2021.[107]

In chapter 9, I'll offer some broad thoughts on the military posture of the United States as regards the challenge from Moscow and Beijing, but here let me offer a different closing thought: to confront successfully the hostile powers in Beijing and Moscow, the United States must strengthen partnerships with its allies. Unfortunately, Donald Trump has presided over a deterioration of these relationships on a scale that I don't find comparable to any postwar American administration. The positions he has taken on issues of geostrategic importance have often been at odds with our allies' understanding of these situations. He infamously mocked NATO as "obsolete," a statement that reverberated around the world, troubling millions in Europe and making many wonder whether Trump truly understood the significance of NATO in the postwar world. Trump's evident contempt for the alliance system and the requirements it imposes on the United States has been evident from his first day in office, as his withdrawal from a series of arms control treaties has made clear—decisions that make our allies more vulnerable.

Trump's withdrawal from the Open Skies Treaty in 2020 is a good example. Open Skies permits dozens of countries to

---

107   Rempfer, Kyle. "Soldiers in Europe for Defender 2020 to return home amid pandemic." Army Times, 16 Mar. 2020, https://www.armytimes.com/news/your-army/2020/03/16/soldiers-in-europe-for-defender-2020-to-return-home-amid-pandemic-2/.

conduct unarmed surveillance of one another, with the goal of improving transparency and lessening the chances of open military conflict. The administration cited Russia's violations—Moscow has not been permitting flights over areas where military exercises take place—in announcing its decision to leave the treaty. But America's allies, including France, Germany, and Poland, did not feel that the Russian violations rose to the level of seriousness that would warrant this action, and I concur with that judgment. It is yet another move by the Trump administration that weakens our alliances at a time when we need to be strengthening them. The most effective way for the United States to counter Russian aggression is close partnership with our European allies. Leaving the Open Skies agreement only sows more division between America and Europe—precisely the result that Putin seeks.

Trump's departure from Open Skies is just another exhibit of his scattered foreign policy, one in which America seems to lack overarching commitments to its partners, whether in Europe or elsewhere, but is rather guided by the erratic impulses and inconsistent decision-making priorities of the president. Faced with a mounting challenge from an adversarial axis, the United States needs not just a well-considered military response and strategic vision: it needs much better leadership.

CHAPTER SIX

Rogue States

T HE BURGEONING MILITARY POWER OF RUSSIA AND CHINA is even more troubling in the context of their longstanding support for the world's most notorious rogue states, especially North Korea and Iran.

North Korea

No one disputes that China is central to North Korea's existence. Without Beijing, the regime in Pyongyang would surely collapse, and this has been the case for long before the arrival of Kim Jong-un. China's support of North Korea dates to the Korean War, when the People's Liberation Army backstopped the North's war against its southern enemy and the United States. Ever since, Beijing and Pyongyang have been locked in a difficult embrace, but no one seriously thinks that the Chinese will let go—too much rides on the North's survival and stability.

Thus China continues to provide essential diplomatic assistance and economic support for Pyongyang—in addition to "technology, components, equipment, and materials for its nuclear weapons and ballistic missile programs," as Gordon Chang points out, "all the while claiming that it's taming the beast."[108]

It starts with economics. China is North Korea's largest trading partner by far. Without China, the North would not survive; without China, in fact, Pyongyang couldn't even keep its lights on. Beijing supplies almost all North Korea's oil and apparently sells this fuel at prices that it calibrates according to its assessments of Pyongyang's stability, not UN dictates as regards economic sanctions.[109] Beijing accounts for almost the entirety—some 90 percent—of the North Korean export market. Trade between the two nations increased tenfold in the decade and a half between 2000 and 2015. The growth has slowed somewhat since the UN imposed $1 billion in sanctions on the North in 2017 after its missile tests, but Beijing played along only reluctantly—and partially. "China spiked its imports of cheap North Korean coal just before the deadline," writes Ariel Cohen in *Forbes*, pointing out that later that summer, "China purchased $138 million worth of the commodity when monthly averages typically hover under $90 million."[110]

Even as trade dropped off in the wake of the sanctions, evidence suggests that "informal trade" between the two nations

---

108   Chang, Gordon. "Here's How China Plays North Korea—And Trump." The Daily Beast, 14 Mar. 2019, https://www.thedailybeast.com/heres-how-china-plays-north-koreaand-trump?ref=scroll.

109   Easley, Leif-Eric. "Why China Takes a Middle-of-the-Road Policy toward North Korea." Washington Post, 28 Feb. 2019, https://www.washingtonpost.com/politics/2019/02/28/why-china-takes-middle-of-the-road-policy-toward-north-korea/.

110   Cohen, Ariel. "North Korea Illegally Trades Oil, Coal, With China's Help." Forbes, 21 Mar. 2019, https://www.forbes.com/sites/arielcohen/2019/03/21/north-korea-illegally-trades-oil-coal-with-chinas-help/#2ff68304301a.

is growing, as Beijing helps the Kim regime facilitate imports into the country through non-approved channels. A 2018 UN report found China a central player in helping North Korea evade sanctions on its oil and coal trade. The report cited "nearly 300 foreign businesses and individuals, including 215 from China and 39 from Russia, that have allegedly flouted sanctions by forming prohibited joint ventures with North Koreans," according to a report in *Foreign Policy*.[111]

(China also expressed solidarity with North Korea during the pandemic, with Xi voicing his nation's willingness to "continue to provide assistance within its own capacity for [North Korea] in the fight against Covid-19."[112] To date, North Korea has no official cases of the virus, though many believe that it has entered the country. And when Kim fell mysteriously ill for several weeks in spring 2020—with some speculation, unverified, that he might have the virus—a Chinese medical team was sent to Pyongyang.)

In June 2019, a U.S. judge found three large Chinese banks in contempt for "refusing to comply with subpoenas in an investigation into North Korean sanctions violations."[113] The U.S. held that the banks had "knowingly helped finance North Ko-

---

111   Lynch, Colum. "U.N. Report Details How North Korea Evades Sanctions." Foreign Policy, 20 Sept. 2019, https://foreignpolicy.com/2018/09/20/un-report-details-how-north-korea-evades-sanctions/.

112   "China Offers to Help North Korea Fight Pandemic." BBC News, 9 May 2020, https://www.bbc.com/news/world-asia-52597749

113   "US Judge Holds Three Chinese Banks in Contempt for Refusing to Comply with Probes into Violations of North Korea Sanction." South China Morning Post, 25 June 2019, https://www.scmp.com/business/banking-finance/article/3015938/us-judge-holds-three-chinese-banks-contempt-refusing.

rea's nuclear-proliferation network"[114] by working with a Hong Kong front company to launder more than $100 million for North Korea's Foreign Trade Bank. The order could lead to the exclusions of the Chinese banks from the U.S. financial system.

Much of the official trade between Beijing and Pyongyang flows through the Chinese border city of Dandong, just across the Yalu River from North Korea, and described as "North Korea's lifeline to the outside world."[115] By some estimates, the black-market economy is larger than the official trade. A 2013 report found that the North Korean elite can get whatever they want at Dandong, ranging from "luxury food and fine wine" and "Apple iMacs for Kim Jong-un" to "Chinese-built missile launchers and components for their nuclear arsenal."[116]

It's bad enough that China has helped the North flout international sanctions, thus eroding their effectiveness—but the assistance, by keeping the North Korean economy afloat, also helps the Kim regime pursue the very aims that prompted the sanctions: development of its nuclear program. Here, again, China is the key player, and while it clearly would like to see North Korea dial down its nuclear adventurism, Beijing has

---

114 Hsu, Spencer S. "Chinese Bank Involved in Probe on North Korean Sanctions and Money Laundering Faces Financial 'Death Penalty.'" Washington Post, 24 June 2019, https://www.washingtonpost.com/local/legal-issues/chinese-bank-involved-in-probe-on-north-korean-sanctions-and-money-laundering-faces-financial-death-penalty/2019/06/22/0ccef3ba-81be-11e9-bce7-40b4105f7ca0_story.html.

115 Moore, Malcolm. "China Breaking UN Sanctions to Support North Korea." The Telegraph, 13 Apr. 2013, https://www.telegraph.co.uk/news/worldnews/asia/northkorea/9991907/China-breaking-UN-sanctions-to-support-North-Korea.html.

116 Moore, Malcolm. "China Breaking UN Sanctions to Support North Korea." The Telegraph, 13 Apr. 2013, https://www.telegraph.co.uk/news/worldnews/asia/northkorea/9991907/China-breaking-UN-sanctions-to-support-North-Korea.html.

also enabled it. Rather than consistently pushing the North toward full denuclearization as the best path to international acceptance and integration, Beijing plays a double game—pressing the North when the political climate dictates but working behind the scenes otherwise to assist the regime in its pursuits. North Korea is likely reconstituting its rocket and missile facilities, for instance: in March 2019, South Korean surveillance revealed that the North was restoring the facilities of a long-range rocket site that had been disassembled as part of a disarmament agreement.[117]

It's not just nukes that the Chinese are helping with. "The Chinese military supports North Korea's dangerous weaponization efforts to the hilt," Gordon Chang wrote in 2017.[118] Chang pointed out how a new North Korean missile, displayed at a military parade that year, looked different from anything else the North Koreans had shown before. Specifically, the canister containing it closely resembled the one that China uses for its DF-31 missile, which has a range of at least 5,000 miles—and could reach the United States if launched from the northeastern part of North Korea. The missile that the North Koreans *did* launch in 2017 looked to experts a lot like China's Jl-1 ballistic missile, fired from submarines. And this comes on top of what we definitively know: that China transferred KN-08 mobile

---

117   Kim, Hyung-Jin, and Kim Tong-Hyung. "North Korea Said to Be Rebuilding Structures at Rocket Site." Associated Press, 6 Mar. 2019, https://apnews.com/415b-f87602bf41bea1a9034245560ac6.

118   Chang, Gordon. "Is China Really Abandoning North Korea?" Forbes, 16 Apr. 2017, https://www.forbes.com/sites/gordonchang/2017/04/16/is-china-really-abandoning-north-korea/#3fb049812f1c.

missile launchers to North Korea. The KN-08 is a missile with the capacity to strike the American homeland.

Would Beijing stand by Pyongyang, militarily, in the case of a military conflict with the United States? A 1961 treaty between the two countries binds China to intervene if the North is subject to deliberate or unprovoked aggression—obviously, how such designations are defined would be crucial. The Chinese have also suggested, however, that their treaty obligations would not apply if it were the North that initiated hostilities. In any case, in such an event, there is no doubt that Beijing would seek to shape events.

A few years ago, a retired Chinese military officer said of his country's relationship with the Hermit Kingdom: "North Korea is a rabid dog we have in a large cage."[119] China often finds that the cage is not secure or large enough, but it understands that keeping the totalitarian regime stable is in its best interests: avoiding regime collapse is a governing priority. Keeping the Korean Peninsula divided, and remaining an ally of North Korea, helps China maintain its authority in the region. Avoiding regime collapse forestalls other problems that China doesn't want on its doorstep—principally, a huge refugee influx, but also the geopolitical gain that North Korea's demise would represent for Japan, South Korea, and the United States. Beijing's ally in Pyongyang is frequently exasperating, but an unpredictable North Korea keeps the United States off balance.

------

119   Chang, Gordon. "Here's How China Plays North Korea—And Trump." The Daily Beast, 14 Mar. 2019, https://www.thedailybeast.com/heres-how-china-plays-north-koreaand-trump.

In short, China has never abandoned Pyongyang. It continues to supply the Hermit Kingdom with weaponry, economic aid, and diplomatic cover.

◆ ◆ ◆

North Korea does not enjoy this same level of support from Moscow, to be sure, but Russia has sought a deepened relationship in recent years. The supply of Russian oil has become essential to North Korean survival. And Russia's expertise in missile technology has now become an important factor in North Korea's nuclear-weapons quest.

This became clear in summer 2017, when North Korea fired an ICBM with the range to hit Alaska, according to assessments. This was the incident that prompted President Trump's infamous tweets about raining "fire and fury" down on Pyongyang. The test came as an alarm to North Korea watchers, since it seemed to represent a major progression in its efforts to develop missile technology. Up until then, the North's missile-firing efforts were long on rhetoric and short on results, often prompting ridicule in the West.

Yet here, Kim Jong Un suddenly revealed a capacity to fire at least a plausible missile, with a plausible range. How had the North made such an advance so quickly, without any apparent warning? Not long afterward, a *New York Times* report provided part of the answer: The North Koreans had upgraded their ballistic-missile capabilities by purchasing, on the black market, "powerful rocket engines probably from a Ukrainian factory with historical ties to Russia's missile program."[120] During the Cold War, the Ukrainian factory had made the Soviet Union's most lethal missiles. The Russian tie was made more explicit by U.S. analysts' conclusion, after inspecting photos of the missiles' rocket motors, that their technology reflected old Soviet designs. The Americans believed that the motors had enough power that "a single missile could hurl 10 thermonuclear warheads between continents."

Putin has defended the North Korean nuclear program as self-defensive. From his perspective, the nukes, or the threat of nukes, guarantee the security of Kim's regime by serving as a deterrent against regime change. And Putin wants stability in North Korea more than he wants anything else. Like Xi, he does not want a North Korean refugee crisis on his eastern border. It is likely as well that he sees Kim's nuclear efforts as a way of keeping China honest, too; it is all in keeping with Putin's broader approach, seen with rogue states as well as in his dealings in the Middle East generally, of pursuing a balance of power that redounds primarily to Russia's benefit.

Putin has shown willingness to express his support for Kim with high-profile demonstrations of military capability. In April 2017, when tensions ran high between Washington and Pyongyang, Putin massed troops along the Russia-North Korea border. Not long after the *Times*'s revelations about the Ukrainian missile factory, on a day when the United States and South Korea were conducting joint military exercises, Putin flew nuclear bombers over the Korean Peninsula.

-----

120   Broad, William J., and David E. Sanger. "North Korea's Missile Success Is Linked to Ukrainian Plant, Investigators Say." The New York Times, 14 Aug. 2017, https://www.nytimes.com/2017/08/14/world/asia/north-korea-missiles-ukraine-factory.html.

Moscow is adept at working closely with its Chinese partners to tamp down international efforts to discipline Pyongyang. Several months after the "fire and fury episode," the North detonated a device underground that Kim claimed was a hydrogen bomb—one that could be put on an ICBM and reach the United States. The UN responded swiftly with sanctions; though these were the toughest yet levied on the North, Russia, with Chinese help, ensured that the sanctions were weakened seriously. Moscow and Beijing eroded the original sanctions language, which contemplated ending oil imports to North Korea, in favor of merely capping them at current levels. Once the sanctions were watered down, Moscow and Beijing voted for them—projecting the image of getting tough on Kim, while doing what was necessary to ensure his survival.

Moscow has failed to uphold other UN economic sanctions against North Korea, including allegedly lending its facilities to Pyongyang so that it could ship coal to Japan and South Korea. About 10,000 North Korean laborers continue to work in Russia, in violation of international efforts to prevent Pyongyang from earning foreign currency from labor abroad.[121]

These moves are largely economic, from Moscow's perspective. The Kremlin is looking for economic opportunities on the Korean Peninsula, pursuing a wide-ranging plan to boost its economic presence in Asia, which includes a revived proposal to build a gas pipeline through North Korea. And Moscow has no more interest in seeing the Kim regime fall than Beijing

---

121 Snyder, Scott A. "Where Does the Russia-North Korea Relationship Stand?" Council on Foreign Relations, 29 Apr. 2019, https://www.cfr.org/in-brief/where-does-russia-north-korea-relationship-stand.

does. While Moscow isn't keen on North Korea as a nuclear power, the Russians do see the utility in the North having a limited nuclear capacity, as a check against international attempts at regime change.

The Russians are even more likely to see things that way given the recent U.S. withdrawal from the Open Skies Treaty, which allows dozens of countries to conduct unarmed surveillance of one another, enhancing transparency and lessening the risk of military conflicts. As I noted in Chapter 5, the Trump administration withdrew from the treaty citing violations by Russia, but in doing so it has left our European allies with less protection and coordination. U.S. withdrawal will likely also embolden rogue nations like North Korea. Under Trump, the U.S. has pulled out from several major arms control agreements. Both the rogue nations and Russia will be encouraged to augment their own programs in this context, and Russia could become increasingly permissive of North Korean nuclear developments (and, for that matter, similar efforts in Iran).

As Putin sees it, "Kim Jong-un has learned from the fates of Iraq's Saddam Hussein and Libya's Col. Muammar el-Qaddafi that for an authoritarian regime, the only safeguard against U.S. military intervention is the possession of nuclear weapons capable of hitting the American mainland," says Aleksandr Gabuev, a fellow at the Moscow Carnegie Center.[122] And Russia, too, wants no part of a refugee crisis that would result from a violent or disorderly collapse of the Kim regime.

---

122   Snyder, Scott A. "Where Does the Russia-North Korea Relationship Stand?" Council on Foreign Relations, 29 Apr. 2019, https://www.cfr.org/in-brief/where-does-russia-north-korea-relationship-stand.

Putin, cagey as ever, has watched the Trump administration's on-again, off-again attempts at reconciliation with Pyongyang. After the Trump-Kim summit in Vietnam failed, Russia quickly announced a scheduled meeting between Kim and Putin, in Vladivostok. Though the meeting was largely symbolic and did not produce any key developments, it demonstrated Russia's growing interest in becoming a player in the ongoing international struggle over North Korean denuclearization.

As for North Korea itself, even the coronavirus could not tamp down its provocative behavior. In late March 2020, with a substantial portion of the global population living under lockdown to minimize the spread of the virus, Kim Jong Un fired two short-range missiles into the sea off the eastern coast of North Korea. The missiles did no damage, and, at a time when the global community had much else to worry about, did not garner many headlines. But they served as a reminder, if any were needed, about the nature of the regime in Pyongyang.

Iran

When it comes to the world's other key rogue nation—Iran— the roles are reversed, with Russia holding the deeper ties and China more of a junior partner. Russian-Iranian cooperation is ironic in many respects, given the history of enmity between the two in the twentieth century and throughout the Cold War. Not anymore. "Russia is now Iran's most important ally," says Ali Vaez of the International Crisis Group.[123] All the more so in the Trump years, when the U.S. has withdrawn from the Iran

---

123   New Yorker article

nuclear deal and provided new openings for a Moscow-Tehran relationship.

"Our cooperation can isolate America," Iran's Supreme Leader Ali Khamenei told Putin in November 2017, when the Russian president flew to Tehran for talks. Putin called Russian-Iranian cooperation "very productive."[124] Putin's message to Khamenei, according to Vaez, was: "I will not betray you."[125] That's a pledge that would interest the Iranians, since, over the last 20 years, Moscow has let them down more than once—each time as a result of trying to forge a closer relationship with Washington. Moscow's hopes were dashed, in the 1990s, when promised economic assistance from America didn't materialize, and, more recently, when U.S.-Russian relations soured over Ukraine.

Russian-Iranian military ties have been strengthening for years. In Syria, the two nations' military cooperation had long been coordinated by Qasem Soleimani, leader of the élite Quds Force, Iran's rough equivalent to U.S. Special Operations Forces, before he was killed in the Trump-ordered U.S. attack in January 2020 (which Russia quickly deemed illegal). The Quds has backed terrorist groups including Hezbollah, Hamas, and Palestinian Islamic Jihad. General Valery Gerasimov, chief of staff of the Russian armed forces, has gone to Tehran to meet with his counterpart, Iranian Major General Mohammad Bagheri, who oversees all branches of the Iranian military, including its Revolutionary Guards.

---

124   ibid
125   ibid

The Russian/Iranian relationship has many components. Economically, the two countries have a trade relationship worth about $4 billion annually, much of it in military goods. Russia is Iran's biggest source of foreign weapons, helping modernize its defenses (and keeping the Russian military-industrial sector busy). Russia is a key deflector of punitive sanctions against Iran proposed by the U.S. and its allies at the United Nations.

But the nuclear alliance, which dates to the 1990s, is the most troubling aspect. Iran's Bushehr reactor, situated on the Persian Gulf coast, wouldn't exist without Russia. Its construction, development, and operation are the product of decades' worth of Iranian cooperation with the Russian business and scientific establishments. And Russia is helping the Iranians build a second reactor there. Meanwhile, clandestine Russian involvement has been essential to Iran's development of a heavy-water reactor in Arak, which, at full capacity, will be capable of producing weapons-grade plutonium. The Russian nuclear-energy firm, Rosatom, operates the Bushehr plant, supplies all fuel from Russian sources, and processes and disposes of spent fuel in Russia.[126]

Significant tensions do exist. The Russians are the main benefactors of the deterioration in Iran-U.S. relations, since it plays into their overarching narrative about American meddling in the Middle East, but also, more substantively, because other countries can't buy Iranian oil without worrying about repercussions from Washington—and that means that they're more likely to buy Russian oil. Further, the chilling of relations

126 "Iran Begins Loading Bushehr Nuclear Reactor." BBC, 21 Aug. 2010, https://www.bbc.com/news/world-middle-east-11045537.

with Washington drives Iran closer into the Russian orbit for assistance, especially for arms and nuclear technology.

Syria, where the two nations have cooperated throughout the civil war, remains volatile, and the two nations face tensions there. "In Syria—just as in any other arena of geopolitical competition—there can be just one hegemon—either Russia or Iran," writes Robert Czulda for the Atlantic Council. "The more problems faced by Iran, the lower the chance that it will be able to prevent Russian dominance in a post-war Syria."[127] Recent tensions include conflicts between Russian and Iranian forces in Syria.

"The disagreements they're having is that they're trying to carve out spheres of influence in Syria, which is something that Russia understands very well," said Anna Borshchevskaya of the European Foundation for Democracy. "Their relationship is a complex one, for sure. But what holds them together is their anti-Americanism and a desire to reduce American influence in the region." That's exactly right, and it is this focus that keeps the two nations working together, as Borshchevskaya herself concedes: "I never believe that Russia would separate from Iran."[128]

And it's worth remembering the remarkably close cooperation between Iran and Russia during the Syrian civil war, in which both countries put all their chips on the table in order

---

127 "Iran Begins Loading Bushehr Nuclear Reactor." BBC, 21 Aug. 2010, https://www.bbc.com/news/world-middle-east-11045537.

128 Kajjo, Sirwan. "Tensions Grow Between Russia, Iran in Syria." Voice of America, 27 May 2019, https://www.voanews.com/extremism-watch/tensions-grow-between-russia-iran-syria.

to preserve the Assad regime—and saw the bet pay off. Iran's coordination with Moscow was so close that it even permitted Russian air force planes to take off from Iranian air bases to conduct bombing operations in Syria. Their alliance was enabled by American timidity, especially by President Obama's infamous walk-back of his so-called red line against Syrian use of chemical weapons in 2013. When Assad used chemical weapons anyway—sarin gas—and Obama, instead of intervening as promised stood down instead, Tehran and Moscow had a green light to proceed.

Russian military intervention in the Syrian civil war got underway in earnest in September 2015, when Putin responded to Assad's request for help in fighting rebel forces and ISIS. Though Putin made a big show, rhetorically, of fighting ISIS, it didn't take long before the Russian priorities became clear: Moscow's initial bombing campaigns were almost entirely directed against the more moderate, anti-Assad rebel factions, what became known as the Free Syrian Army. It is almost unthinkable that Assad could have prevailed in this struggle without Russian assistance—and we will never know whether Putin would have backed off, had Obama delivered on his commitments. What we do know is that the Syrian Civil War was the crucial event, over the last half-decade, that marked a potentially historic transition in the Middle East: Russia was displacing the United States as the region's power broker.

The American retreat in Syria, as elsewhere, has had direct, and devastating effects on human rights and the safety and survival of vulnerable populations. Russia has committed a broad range of human rights violations in Syria, both independently and in tandem with Assad's rogue regime. After a Russian-Syrian bombing campaign against Aleppo in 2016, which killed hundreds of civilians, including children, Human Rights Watch accused the two nations of war crimes. The bombing campaign killed at least 440 civilians, including more than 90 children. Human Rights Watch also alleges that Russia has bombed hospitals—deliberately—and used what it calls "indiscriminate weapons," such as incendiary devices or cluster munitions, not meant for specific military targets.[129]

Russia's entry into these events, along with American acquiescence, was truly transformative in tipping the balance of power. Iran and Syria are historical allies. Iran deploys its Revolutionary Guard troops in Syria, where it also funds Hezbollah, the terrorist group that has long enjoyed the backing of Assad.[130] Yet alone, the two nations likely would not have been able to resist a concerted international effort against Assad. It was Moscow that made the difference.

Russian and Iran, to be sure, are not natural allies, and before recent years, their mutual history was a difficult one, shot through with Cold War tensions and other problems. But their determination to resist the priorities of the United States and its Western allies trumps all misgivings, as the Syrian conflict showed. Russia sees Iran as a key partner, and the Iranians are in no position to turn down Russian backing, whether military, nuclear, or diplomatic. No matter what discord might arise

---

129 "Russia/Syria: War Crimes in Month of Bombing Aleppo," *Human Rights Watch*, 1 December 2016, https://www.hrw.org/news/2016/12/01/russia/syria-war-crimes-month-bombing-aleppo.

130 Fulton, Will et al., "Iranian Strategy in Syria," *Institute for the Study of War*, May 2013, http://www.understandingwar.org/report/iranian-strategy-syria.

between the two countries, they see a common adversary: the United States. Moscow's attitude is best summed up in a remark that scholar Georgy Mirsky once heard a Russian diplomat say: "I would rather have a nuclear Iran than a pro-American Iran."[131] The phrase speaks volumes about the Russian attitude to Tehran.

Russia the Rogue

Finally, it is worth considering whether Russia itself might qualify as a rogue state. After all, Russia has been found officially liable for a chemical weapons attack in a NATO country. In March 2018, former Russian military office Sergei Skripal, a double agent for the U.K., was poisoned, along with his daughter Yulia, in Salisbury, England, by a military-grade nerve agent identified as Novichok. Both Skripal and his daughter eventually recovered, though they spent weeks in critical condition. Several British law enforcement officers were also hospitalized due to exposure to the agent. It was an act not only of horrific violence but also of incredible brazenness—a kind of terrorist attack on British soil, directed by Moscow. The Organization for Prevention of Chemical Weapons ruled Russia guilty in the attack, confirming an earlier British verdict.

Combine this attack with Russia's invasions over the past decade of Georgia and Ukraine. Moscow has backed separatist militias in Ukraine with funding, weaponry, and military

---

131 Ioffe, Julia. "The Cold War Heats Up in Syria." The New Republic, 21 May 2013, https://newrepublic.com/article/113255/syria-why-russia-and-united-states-cant-agree.

support. Some of the militia groups have attacked civilians. In 2018, the head of U.S. forces in Afghanistan told the BBC that Russia was supplying arms to the Taliban. "We know that the Russians are involved," he said.[132]

Then there's Russia's long-running support and enablement of the murderous Assad regime in Syria, itself the perpetrator of numerous war crimes. As part of that effort, in Syria, Russian military forces have collaborated with Lebanese Hezbollah, one of the world's most notorious terrorist organizations. Moreover, Ukrainian reporting suggests that Russia actually provided material support to ISIS in Syria, including assistance with recruitment. Remember that fighting ISIS was the main priority of the United States in Syria. Though Putin wanted to buck up Assad against the Syrian rebels, ISIS were anti-Assad, too. Yet he was willing to help them, to some degree, at least—even as he maintained, through his public statements, that he was joining in the fight against the terrorist group. Moscow's support, according to reports, has resulted in thousands of Russian-speaking jihadis among the ISIS recruits.

Add to all this Russia's active campaign of cyber warfare and sabotage against the United States and other Western democracies, and you have a pretty good case that Russia might qualify for the State Department's State Sponsors of Terrorism list. That's what motivated Senator Cory Gardner of Colorado to introduce legislation in 2018 to require the State Department to make a ruling on whether Russia should be so designated.

---

132   Rowlatt, Justin. "Russia 'Arming the Afghan Taliban', Says US." BBC, 23 Mar. 2018, https://www.bbc.com/news/world-asia-43500299.

That legislation remains pending, but it's worth considering in this context that President Trump pushed to get North Korea designated as a state sponsor of terrorism in 2017, even though State Department officials and other experts didn't find the case very persuasive. But "Russia much more neatly meets the definition of a state sponsor than North Korea does," said a national security official.[133]

If Gardner's legislation is adopted, and the State Department goes on to name Russia a state sponsor of terrorism, would this have any real-world impact? I confess that I don't know. But it would surely represent a conscious and explicit acknowledgement, on the part of the United States, of the role that Russia has been playing in the world as an active destabilizing force and enemy of democratic values. If this were all that the designation accomplished, it would still represent a step forward.

An American Leadership Vacuum

The American response to the rogue threat—the inadequacy of that response, in most cases—has played an enormous role in making that threat harder to contain and more dangerous to address. I'm fully bipartisan in this critique: in my earlier books, I have found the Obama administration's policies wholly inadequate to the situation, whether it concerned the ill-considered Iranian nuclear deal or the ongoing nuclear provocations of Pyongyang. In his own way, Donald Trump is no better.

---

133   Rotella, Sebastian. "The U.S. Considered Declaring Russia a State Sponsor of Terror, Then Dropped It." ProPublica, 21 May 2018, https://www.propublica.org/article/united-states-considered-declaring-russia-a-state-sponsor-of-terror.

His scattershot personal approach to foreign policy—especially his damaging public statements and tweets— has continually undermined American interests in this area, even when his administration has put in writing a coherent approach and top aides pursue sensible goals. Trump's record of volatility and unpredictability puts his entire foreign policy in jeopardy, and nowhere is this danger more pronounced than in dealing with rogue states.

CHAPTER SEVEN

Energy, Economy, and the Third World

CONSIDER THE SCENE AT THE ST. PETERSBURG INTERNA-tional Economic Forum in June 2019, Russia's annual summit. There, Xi and Putin exalted one another, presenting the relationship between their two countries as the best it had ever been. Russia, Xi said, was "not only our largest neighbor and a comprehensive strategic partner, but also one of the most important and most prioritized partners in all areas of coop-eration." Putin said that Russian maintained "very deep and wide-ranging relations with China" and that "we are strategic partners in the fullest sense." Beijing sent a huge delegation to the event—far exceeding the size of the American contingent or that of other Western powers.

Peeling away the diplomatic language, the economic relation-ship is one in which China clearly stands as the dominant part-ner—yet both nations benefit. In 2018, trade between the two topped $100 billion for the first time. The basic breakdown is this: Russia largely sends China raw materials, while the Chinese largely send Russia finished products. Oil and other minerals ac-count for more than three-quarters of Russian exports to China.

Beijing is now Moscow's largest overseas oil market, accounting for a quarter of all Moscow's exports—and that should grow, once the Power of Siberia pipeline is completed. On the other side, Russia largely imports from China finished goods and consumer products—cars, electronics, machinery, shoes, clothing.

It works well for both sides, though Russia is concerned about becoming a raw materials outpost for the Chinese, and the Chinese have made minimal domestic investment in Russia, put off by the volatile Russian business and legal environment. And Russia just isn't the same kind of large market that China can cater to elsewhere—whether Western Europe, the U.S., or other Asian economies.[134]

Still, both countries have become reliable partners in a world less open to free trade. Russia faces constraints from the West due to its actions in Ukraine; China is embroiled in a trade war with the U.S. In a climate where the democratic West imposes penalties on both economies, Moscow and Beijing see one another as business partners.

At the heart of the economic relationship is energy. "The real fundamental relationship between Moscow and Beijing is all about oil and gas, really," writes Kenneth Rapoza in *Forbes*. "Which makes perfect sense. Russia is China's neighbor. Russia has a lot of energy to sell. China needs energy. One plus one equals two."[135]

---

134   Ishikawa, Yohei. "Russia's cozy economic ties with China are not all they seem." Nikkei Asian Review, 4 July 2019, https://asia.nikkei.com/Spotlight/Comment/Russia-s-cozy-economic-ties-with-China-are-not-all-they-seem.

135   Rapoza, Kenneth. "Russia And China Only Look Like They Are Becoming Buddies. It's Mostly Talk." Forbes, 5 Jun 2019, https://www.forbes.com/sites/kenrapoza/2019/06/05/russia-and-china-only-look-like-they-are-becoming-buddies-its-mostly-talk/#43fd64d04f64

In 2014, the two nations closed the biggest gas deal Russia has taken part in since the fall of the Soviet Union. On a two-day visit to Shanghai, Putin oversaw the signing of a 30-year deal between Gazprom and the China National Petroleum Corporation (CNPC), estimated to be worth over $400 billion and stipulating that Russia would route 38 billion cubic meters of gas into China annually.[136] The Power of Siberia pipeline, when completed, will run 4,000 kilometers, through Russia and into Asia.[137] Gazprom is heading up the construction of the pipeline from the Russian side. In September 2018, the Russian side of the line was reported to be near completion and the same held true for the Chinese portion.[138] The entire pipeline could be completed by the end of 2019.[139]

The global outbreak of Covid-19 looks also to be strengthening Putin's position. It has started a global oil-price war between Russia, Saudi Arabia, and the United States, a struggle that the first two nations seem better-positioned to endure, at least for the short term. Many U.S. energy firms could face bankruptcy, the American shale industry will likely suffer enormously—much to Putin's pleasure—and the United States' global energy

136 Luhn, Alec, and Macalister, Terry. "Russia signs 30-year deal worth $400bn to deliver gas to China." The Guardian, 21 May 2014, https://www.theguardian.com/world/2014/may/21/russia-30-year-400bn-gas-deal-china

137 "Beijing wants more Russian gas as Gazprom's mega pipeline to China nears completion." Russia Today, 29 May 2019, https://www.rt.com/business/460519-china-russia-more-gas-supplies/

138 "Beijing wants more Russian gas as Gazprom's mega pipeline to China nears completion." Russia Today, 29 May 2019, https://www.rt.com/business/460519-china-russia-more-gas-supplies/

139 Luhn, Alec, and Macalister, Terry. "Russia signs 30-year deal worth $400bn to deliver gas to China." The Guardian, 21 May 2014, https://www.theguardian.com/world/2014/may/21/russia-30-year-400bn-gas-deal-china

gains of the last decade or so, in which we have made enormous strides to energy independence, may be upended. How it will all unfold remains to be seen, of course, but one can expect that Putin will continue to play his energy hand with skill and ruthlessness, as he has for years.

Russia's energy prowess is crucial for Beijing as it faces possible trade disruptions with the U.S. "Russian exports do not need to be shipped by sea and their value in times of possible disruption are difficult to underestimate," writes political analyst Dmitriy Frolovskiy. Further, he points out, "The Russian style of political leadership is also more familiar to Beijing. Therefore, doing business and assuring delivery with state-run corporations such as Gazprom or the privately owned Sibur, of which a 10 per cent stake is owned by Chinese Sinopec and another 10 per cent by the Silk Road Fund, seems easier and more reliable" than depending on resolution of issues with the U.S. or the other Western democracies.

So solid is the reciprocal relationship at this point that Russia does not even raise a voice—at least, not publicly—about a Chinese development and expansion plan that might be the most ambitious ever conceived, one that spreads far enough to encroach on Russia's "near abroad": the Belt and Road Initiative. The BRI was launched in 2013 by Xi Jinping while he was on a trip to Kazakhstan and Indonesia. The first piece, the land portion, or "belt"—or what Xi calls the "Silk Road economic belt"—connects China to the rest of Asia and to Europe. The "belt" terminology is meant to imply a deep network of connection, from infrastructure to economic relations. The maritime component of the massive project, though the "maritime Silk Road," involves deeper ties between port cities in the

South China Sea and those in the Indian Ocean and Mediter-ranean Sea.

Xi envisioned the plan to create a network of railways and roads that would connect nearly every country in Asia, for China to expand its economy, its political influence, and the reach of its renminbi currency. More than 60 countries have signed onto the BRI, representing two-thirds of the world's population and accounting for one-third of global GDP. Virtually every country in Asia and Eastern Europe is a part of it. Egypt, Sudan, Ethiopia, Kenya, Tanzania, South Africa, and Djibouti have signed on, too, from Africa. Morgan Stanley predicted that the total cost of the BRI could be $1.2 trillion to 1.3 trillion by 2027.[140] It is a project of unrivaled immensity in recent history. The BRI's targeted completion date is 2049.

Xi calls it the "project of the century," and it's hard to disagree. What could possibly rival Belt & Road for size, scale, and ambition? Though the World Bank calls it, using its best internationalist, value-neutral language, a "China-led effort to improve connectivity and regional co-operation on a trans-continental scale through large-scale investments," the Belt & Road is nothing less than a Chinese reimagining of the world order as a China-directed bloc of economic partners, all buying and selling Chinese goods, and all subject to the heavy influence, economically and sometimes politically, of Chinese authoritarianism. And the project's implications extend beyond the political and economic to encompass the very notion of physical space. As *The Economist* put it, aptly:

---

140   Chatzky, Andrew, and McBride, James. "China's Massive Belt and Road Initiative." Council on Foreign Relations, 28 January 2020, https://www.cfr.org/back-grounder/chinas-massive-belt-and-road-initiative

It is reshaping the geography of the Earth's biggest land mass. In this new space, the obstacles of the recent past—the Iron Curtain, China locked in its Mao-made autarky, even the physical impediments of the Himalayas, the Inner Asian deserts and the melting Arctic itself—are of diminishing consequence. The physical and psychological distance between Europe and East Asia is shrinking as the sparsely populated expanse at the heart of Eurasia is being wrangled, through new infrastructure, to manageable size. That, at least, is how Chinese planners see it. And, taking the historical view, if there is a surprise, it is that the transformation is not being made in the West's image or according to its rules. Asia is coming to Europe, not the other way around.[141]

As noted above, the BRI is split into two parts: the "Belt" of railways and transcontinental highways, and the "Road," a network of maritime ports and sea routes connecting major trade centers. The BRI includes over 100 projects, but five stand out:

- 12,000-kilometer Chinese rail link to Europe, from Yiwu to London;

- China-Pakistan economic corridor, the BRI's biggest single project, with some $54 billion of infrastructure projects;

- Chinese rail link to Iran;

- Central Asian gas pipeline to connect the Caspian Sea to Western China through Kazakhstan;

141   Ziegler, Dominic. "China wants to put itself back at the centre of the world." The Economist, 6 February 2020, https://www.economist.com/special-report/2020/02/06/china-wants-to-put-itself-back-at-the-centre-of-the-world

- and the Khorgos Gateway, a railway-exchange and standardization project involving a city on the Kazak-China border that, with BRI trade, will soon become the world's largest dry port in the world.[142] Xi considers it a crucial part of what he calls the "Eurasian land bridge."

The BRI hit some rough patches in recent years, when internal critics complained that the projects were too costly; a temporary pullback resulted, but now the BRI seems back on the front-burner, with China signing $128 billion in project commitments in 2018. The new projects include everything from a telecom data center in Nairobi to a subway system for Belgrade.

The Covid-19 pandemic will present its own challenges here, as it does in most other areas, but it's highly unlikely that the coronavirus will lead Beijing to pull back substantially from Belt and Road, even in the short term. As Michael Auslin points out, Beijing has multiple options for targeting projects, whether it's developing nations seeking the investment or established European states, like Italy or Greece, facing major financial challenges. China also founded and leads the increasingly powerful Asian Infrastructure Investment Bank, which now numbers perhaps 90 nations as members (counts differ) and is regarded as a serious rival to the World Bank and International Monetary Fund. As Auslin points out, Beijing can use the AIIB "as well as international organizations run or influenced by Chinese officials, such as the UN's International Telecom-

---

142 "The five main projects of the Belt and Road Initiative: A visual explainer." South China Morning Post, https://multimedia.scmp.com/news/china/article/One-Belt-One-Road/index.html

munications Union, Beijing will continue to push forward with favorable deals for Chinese companies, like Huawei, part of a pattern of using IGOs to push state goals."[143]

Beijing has always spun the Belt & Road initiative as an infrastructure-development project, especially with an eye toward the developing world, and there is some truth in that description—as far as it goes. The problem is that China is increasingly running the project in a financially predatory manner, especially for Third World countries in which some projects are located. The construction projects are carried out by Chinese companies and usually financed, through debt, by Chinese banks. The borrowing countries must pay back these loans, either through currency or through oil or other natural resources. Beijing has played hardball with those who can't pay: in 2018, Sri Lanka, unable to pay back its loans, surrendered its main port to Chinese control. Many of China's poor-country partners in the Belt & Road initiative have found themselves facing steeper debt burdens as a result of their participation in the project.

Even the Belt & Road's First World partners have found themselves exploited, usually through anti-competitive practices that the Chinese have set up. A European Chamber of Commerce report found that European shipping firms and other businesses found it hard to compete effectively under the Chinese system. As a report in the *New York Times* explained, "the new ports are designed and managed by Chinese state-owned

------

143   Auslin, Michael R. "The Coronacrisis Will Simply Exacerbate The Geo-Strategic Competition Between Beijing And Washington." Hoover Institution, 23 Apr. 2020, https://www.hoover.org/research/coronacrisis-will-simply-exacerbate-geo-strategic-competition-between-beijing-and

enterprises that are under the same Chinese government agency as Chinese shipbuilders and Chinese shipping companies."[144] And European firms have grown increasingly concerned by China's telecom dominance in developing-world, where two huge Chinese firms, Huawei and ZTE, have penetrated deeply and become formidable players.

Considering how the BRI is clearly an attempt by China to tap into opportunities in Eurasia, portions of which are historic areas of Russian influence, Moscow's attitude has been remarkably supportive. In developing the BRI, Xi has "built an important platform for expanding international cooperation," Putin has said. And Russia was "willing to strengthen exchanges and cooperation, and work with China in energy, connectivity and other major projects." For his part, Xi called Russia "an important partner in co-building the Belt and Road Initiative."

Putin has also praised the BRI in the context of his own pet economic-development initiative, the Eurasian Economic Union (EAEU), an organization of states in central and northern Asia and Eastern Europe. "Countries gathering under the Belt and Road Initiative and EAEU share long-term strategic interests of peace and growth," Putin said.[145] His EAEU is regarded by many observers as a merely symbolic instrument of Russian influence, not as a genuine economic union.

_____

144 Bradsher, Keith. "China Renews Its 'Belt and Road' Push for Global Sway." New York Times, 15 Jan. 2020, https://www.nytimes.com/2020/01/15/business/china-belt-and-road.html

145 Jeong-ho, Lee. "China and Russia forge stronger Eurasian economic ties as Vladimir Putin gets behind Xi Jinping's belt and road plan in face of US hostility." South China Morning Post, 26 Apr. 2019, https://www.scmp.com/news/china/diplomacy/article/3007883/china-and-russia-forge-stronger-eurasian-economic-ties.

That's not the case, though, when it comes to the Shanghai Cooperation Organization (SCO), a major political and economic alliance formed in 2001 and designed to challenge American hegemony in Central and East Asia. Its founding members are China, Russia, Kazakhstan, Kyrgyzstan, Tajikistan, and Uzbekistan, but the pact has expanded its members and mission—to the economic benefit of Russia and China. Many SCO countries are now involved in the BRI. And Russia wants to use the SCO to try to expand the Eurasia Economic Union. Any doubt that the SCO was a major player on the global stage was dispelled when India and Pakistan became members.

Finally, there is the matter of the two countries' penetration into the Arctic, where both have found a new energy base. Russia sees opportunity in the melting north. As the polar caps ebb away, Moscow explores new trade routes through the soon to be open waters. Off Russia's northern coast, China has set out to drill for natural gas.

Russia and China have joined forces in the Maritime Arctic joint venture, an agreement between private companies in both countries to break through the melting arctic ice to clear the way for trade. So far, the four companies involved are Novatek and Sovcomflot (Russia) and the China Ocean Shipping Group (COSCO) and the Silk Road Fund Co. (China). Novatek, Russia's second-largest gas company, pairs with Sovcomflot for transport of LNG. From the Chinese side, COSCO is a government-owned shipping company backed by the investments of the Silk Road Fund. In 2018, the Chinese government published its first official Arctic policy white paper, arguing that Chinese companies should take advantage of opportunities in the region.

The passage of cargo ships through the Arctic ice—a clear expansion of the Sino-Russian global sphere of influence—has raised red flags for the United States. In 2019, for the first time, the Pentagon included a section on the Arctic in its annual report on Chinese military action. American defense planners fear that China could soon deploy nuclear submarines. In May, at the Arctic Council Meeting in Finland, Secretary of State Mike Pompeo called China's actions in the region "aggressive behavior."

The Russia-China offensive in the Arctic presents a major new front in the unfolding cold war between the Beijing/Moscow axis and its Western adversaries. To extract resources in the Arctic, the United States and its partners rely on exclusive economic zones (EEZs), which in turn depend on freedom of navigation through the region's international waters. With a mounting Russian and Chinese presence in those waters, conflict is all but inevitable. David Auerswald and Terry L. Anderson put it well in an article in *The Hill*: "From a power-politics perspective, Chinese and Russian actions in the Arctic put U.S. security and economic interests at risk."[146]

Third World Expansion

From the time the Communist Party came into power in 1949, China made investments throughout Africa. Since the end of the Cold War, China stepped up its involvement, especially in the

---

146   Auerswald, David, and Anderson, Terry L. "China, Russia move into the Arctic—and put US at risk." The Hill, 14 May 2019, https://thehill.com/opinion/national-security/443324-china-russia-move-into-the-arctic-and-put-us-at-risk

form of construction and investment. In 2018, China pledged $600 billion to Africa during the Forum on China-Africa Cooperation. Nearly 12% of Africa's total industrial production is now backed directly by Chinese firms. Chinese-African trade has been growing at a rate of approximately 20% per year, with China being the continent's largest source of construction financing.

A big part of China's interest in Africa is Beijing's need for natural resources to fuel its booming economy, especially oil. By 2020, China will import more oil than any nation in the world. By partnering with oil-rich African nations like Sudan, Angola, and Nigeria, China looks to guarantee future energy supply—while also seeking to make Africa a market for its industrial economy.

In July 2019, 54 African nations met to agree on an international free-trade zone, aiming to tie together 1.3 billion people in a $3.4 trillion trade bloc—the African Continental Free Trade Area. In the works for four years, AfCFTA marks the continent's largest trade deal to date—and China has acted as a broker, signing trade agreements with more than 40 African countries. These agreements reached their peak in 2014, amounting to more than $220 billion in commerce.[147]

Over the last decade, China has established a strong digital presence in the African economy. Two Chinese companies, Huawei and Transsion, now control close to half of the African handset market. Huawei is the biggest developer of 5G technologies in the area and the provider of its most popular handsets.

------

147   Shao, Grace. "What you should know about Africa's massive, 54-country trade bloc." CNBC, 11 July 2019, https://www.cnbc.com/2019/07/11/africa-free-trade-what-is-the-afcfta.html

These Chinese firms have essentially blocked American efforts in the African digital market, in part through their use of extensive customer-research centers, located in Nigeria and Kenya.

Some observers think that China's involvement in Africa rivals older European attempts at colonization. Former Zambian president Michael Sata argues that "European colonial exploitation in comparison to Chinese exploitation appears benign, because even though the commercial exploitation was just as bad, the colonial agents also invested in social and economic infrastructure services. Chinese investment, on the other hand, is focused on taking out of Africa as much as can be taken out, without any regard to the welfare of the local people."[148]

This quasi-imperialist approach is exemplified by China's use of what observers call "debt traps." Under these policies, China will lend massive sums of money to nations, often for infrastructure projects. China has low standards for loan eligibility, often providing countries with loans that are impossible to repay. If a country defaults on its debt, China will use that as leverage to serve political, economic, or military ends.

Consider a Chinese-funded railway in Kenya, for example, from the capital of Nairobi to the port city of Mombasa, offering easy access to the Red Sea via the Gulf of Aden and the Indian Ocean—the largest infrastructure project in Kenyan history. But Kenya currently owes China $5.3 billion, $3.2 billion of which is a loan for the railway project. If Kenya can't pay, China might seize the port of Mombasa—gaining a vital strategic presence

148   Mourdoukoutas, Panos. "What Is China Doing In Africa?", Forbes, 4 Aug. 2018, https://www.forbes.com/sites/panosmourdoukoutas/2018/08/04/china-is-treating-af-rica-the-same-way-european-colonists-did/

allowing it to expand its naval influence farther west. Dependence on Chinese loans is coming back to bite other countries, like Ethiopia and Kenya. Ethiopian loans were structured to be paid off in 15 to 30 years in 2018, but the country has struggled to keep up with payments.

"China is using its rising economic power to build political 'soft power,' says Ted Bauman, Senior Research Analyst at Banyan Hill Publishing. Most of the nations that China partners with recognize and support Beijing's One China Policy as regards Taiwan—a clear success for China in normalizing a critical policy.[149] And it's not all soft power, either— in 2017, China surprised the world by announcing that it was opening its first overseas military base in Djibouti.

In the Western Hemisphere, China has also made inroads. As with its expansion into Africa, Chinese involvement in Latin America is, in large part, an economic endeavor. In 2000, Chinese trade with the region was valued at just $12 billion per year. In 2018, the trade between China and Latin America had grown some 25 times, measuring at $306 billion. Chinese loans to Latin America have now surpassed those made by the World Bank or Inter-American Development bank. Brazil and Venezuela have been the two largest recent recipients of Chinese largesse.[150]

Most of the loans and investment are for financing and infrastructure projects. Energy development is a major focus, too, with Argentina, Chile, and Brazil all pursuing Chinese-fi-

149   Hanauer, Larry, and Morris, Lyle J. "China in Africa: Implications of a Deepening Relationship." Rand Corporation, https://www.rand.org/pubs/research_briefs/RB9760.html

150   Carvalho, Raquel. "China in Latin America: partner or predator?" South China Morning Post, 25 May, 2019, https://multimedia.scmp.com/week-asia/article/3011618/beijing-conquest-latin-america/index.html

nanced hydroelectric projects. Argentina is also reported to be in negotiations with the Chinese to secure funding for an $8 billion nuclear power plant.[151]

China is already Latin America's second-largest trading partner. The U.S. once had hegemonic control of the Western Hemisphere. With a growing Chinese presence, that's no longer the case. Look no further than the statement made by Felipe Henriquez, a successful Latin American technology executive. "Today, we look at China. We look at Meituan, at Alibaba and Tencent, to see what we can do in the future."

China is stepping up its military involvement with Latin America as well. Arms sales from Beijing to Latin America continue to increase, including more advanced and complex systems than ever before—such as surface-to-air missile batteries and personnel carriers. As an arms seller, China holds an advantage in the Latin American defense market: its systems are generally cheaper (though less advanced) than their American or Russian counterparts. And, unlike U.S. or European arms sales, Chinese arms sales are "no strings attached," meaning no need to meet the humanitarian standards the West imposes for its arms sales—preferable for nations like Venezuela, which wouldn't pass muster. And weapons buyers face no limits or restrictions on how they can use the Chinese weapons, another key difference from American and European sellers.[152]

---

151 Carvalho, Raquel. "China in Latin America: partner or predator?" South China Morning Post, 25 May, 2019, https://multimedia.scmp.com/week-asia/article/3011618/beijing-conquest-latin-america/index.html

152 Gurrola, George. "China-Latin America Arms Sales: Antagonizing the United States in the Western Hemisphere?" Military Review, July-August 2018, https://www.armyupress.army.mil/Journals/Military-Review/English-Edition-Archives/July-August-2018/Gurrola-China/

China now has "unprecedented levels of influence and leverage" in Latin America, Admiral Craig Faller, commanding officer of SOUTHCOM, the military combatant command that overseas Latin America, told the Senate Armed Services committee. In Faller's eyes, China is "inside our own neighborhood seeking to displace the United States as the partner of choice and weaken the commitment of our partners to the rule of law and democracy."[153] Chinese increasing presence in the region is even more troubling in the context of Latin America's new wave of leaders, including Michelle Bachelet in Chile, Alan García in Peru, and Lula da Silva in Brazil—all of whom have expressed interest in growing political ties with Beijing.[154]

Just as it has done in Africa, China looks for reciprocity in Latin America in part by persuading allies and partners to cut formal ties with Taiwan. As of April 2019, nine of the 16 countries that still recognize Taiwan are in South America. Yet this number is dwindling: in 2017 and 2018, China persuaded Panama, the Dominican Republic, and El Salvador to switch their recognition from Taiwan to China.[155]

And perhaps most disturbing of all: according to polling done by CADEM, a Chilean firm, China is surpassing the U.S. in popularity in many Latin American countries. In Chile, 77% have a favorable opinion of China, while that number shrinks to 61% for

153 Mehta, Aaron. "What the US needs to counter 'unprecedented' Chinese influence in South America." Defense News, 9 Jul. 2019, https://www.defensenews.com/pentagon/2019/07/09/what-the-us-needs-to-counter-chinese-influence-in-south-america/

154 Lafargue, François. "China's Presence in Latin America." Open Edition Journals, https://journals.openedition.org/chinaperspectives/3053.

155 "China's Engagement with Latin America and the Caribbean." Congressional Research Service, 1 June 2020, https://fas.org/sgp/crs/row/IF10982.pdf.

the United States. In Mexico, China leads the U.S. in favorability by 57% to 43%. In Argentina, 51% see China favorably, compared with 45% who view the U.S. that way. In Peru, China wins the public opinion race by 59% to 56%. In Venezuela, China is ahead, 63% to 62%. U.S. favorability numbers have slipped across the region, even in Brazil and Columbia, where America still leads China.[156]

Latin America is also warming up to Russia, though on a smaller scale. In many ways, the Russia-Latin America relationship is a quid pro quo. Russia assures its allies in Latin America that it will go to bat for them on the UN Security Council when the U.S. and other nations try to punish them for humanitarian violations or political corruption. In exchange, Russia deepens its political ties on a continent that the U.S. regards as its proprietary zone of influence. In an article in *Foreign Affairs Latin America*, Mexican scholar Armando Chaguaceda sums up Russian advantages in approaching the region:

> In Latin America, numerous variables favor the current Russian agenda. In comparison with the United States and Europe, Russia does not have an imperial past with respect to the countries of the Americas. Added to that is the ascendance of anti-American, anti-imperialist political forces throughout Latin America, as well as the neglect of the United States under the Trump administration's policies of isolationism and aggressiveness toward the region.[157]

156 Oppenheimer, Andres. "China is becoming more popular than the U.S. in many Latin American countries." Miami Herald, 24 Apr 2019, https://www.miamiherald.com/news/local/news-columns-blogs/andres-oppenheimer/article229621934.html.

157 Chaguaceda, Armando. "The bear comes to the West: The Russian agenda in Latin America." Global Americans, 20 Mar. 2019, https://theglobalamericans.org/2019/03/the-bear-comes-to-the-west-the-russian-agenda-in-latin-america/.

Along these lines, Chaguaceda says, the Kremlin has "employed various strategies to advance its… broad objectives despite limited resources." Russia enjoys access to Latin American ports and infrastructure, such as the GLONASS satellite station in Nicaragua. Like Venezuela, Nicaragua depends on Russia economically. In Bolivia, Russia has deepened Gazprom's presence.[158] In recent years, Russia has increased sales of military equipment to countries such as Argentina, Colombia, and Mexico, all of whom once bought mostly from the U.S. and Europe. Between 2006 and 2016, trade between Russia and the region increased by 50%. Russian defense officials have discussed opening a permanent military base in Cuba, while also giving Cuba a $50 million loan to buy Russian weapons.

Russia's ties to Venezuela remain its deepest in the region. The political relationship has its roots in the friendship between Putin and Hugo Chavez, the former Communist dictator of Venezuela. After Chavez died in 2013 and Nicolás Maduro took his place, Putin helped Maduro restructure debt while agreeing to invest an additional $6 billion in Venezuela.[159] As he did with Bashar al-Assad in Syria, Putin has stood by Maduro, even as nearly 60 nations now recognize Juan Guaidó, the president of the national assembly, as the country's legitimate ruler. In February 2020, just days after President Trump lauded Guaidó, a personal guest at his State of the Union address, Russian foreign

---

158 Valley, Taylor. "Why Venezuela Needs Russia." The National Interest, 20 June 2019, https://nationalinterest.org/feature/why-venezuela-needs-russia-63472.

159 Gonzalez, Ivelisse. "An Assessment of Russia's Military Presence in Latin America." Foreign Policy Research Institute, 18 June 2019, https://www.fpri.org/article/2019/06/an-assessment-of-russias-military-presence-in-latin-america/

minister Sergei Lavrov met with Maduro, redoubling Moscow's commitment to the embattled ruler.

In late March 2020, the United States indicted Maduro on drug-trafficking charges. The move, the latest in the U.S.'s ongoing effort to force Maduro from power, didn't get a lot of press attention, since it took place when the United States and most other Western nations were in heavy lockdown for the coronavirus. But it is worth reflecting on the fact that, with the long-rumored indictment now official, Russia is now essentially harboring a narcoterrorist from American justice.

Energy, particularly oil, defines the Russia-Venezuela relationship. Rosneft has pumped $14 billion into the Venezuelan gas and oil industry—largely in the hope that Venezuela would maintain its position as South America's primary oil producer. The nation's economic collapse has decimated productivity, however, and Venezuela owes Russia billions. For now, Moscow has chosen to wait out the crisis—but not passively. Rosneft has taken almost total control from PDVSA, Venezuela's state-owned oil company. Russia is clearly determined that Venezuela will pay off its oil debts—and in 2019, Caracas made substantial headway toward doing so, though at great cost. And Venezuelan firms sell steeply discounted oil to Russia, which then sells it on the overseas market, making a tidy profit.

Venezuela remains a key arms buyer from Moscow, too. Chaguaceda reports that "from 2000 to 2010 alone, Moscow sold $11 billion in armaments to Caracas, including fighter-bombers, helicopters, transport planes, heavy tanks, armored cars, artillery, anti-aircraft and anti-submarine systems, radar, transport and logistic vehicles, and firearms." He concludes that "the technology, doctrine and training provided by Moscow are largely responsible for the militarization of Venezuela's internal politics and its possible geopolitical impacts."[160] In January 2019, *Newsweek* reported that Russia flew Tu-160 strategic bombers to Venezuela.[161] The Tu-160 is a nuclear-capable, supersonic bomber.[162]

Russia's media offensive in Latin America is another part of the Putin strategy. Russian news channels are available to Latin Americans via basic cable, and the channels are hiring local correspondents. They're also collaborating with university academics. "Russia Today (RT) and Sputnik Mundo have become sources of information for important segments of the middle and working classes and platforms for anti-liberal populism," Chaguaceda writes. "In all Russian media in the region, Moscow is presented as an alternative of order and development for the region, in stark contrast to the decadent, imperialist West."[163]

In Africa, meanwhile, Russian economic activity pales in comparison to Chinese or European investment—but, like China, Russia is drawn to Africa's vast natural resources. However, whereas Chinese diplomacy and influence is aimed at achieving

---

160 Chaguaceda, Armando. "The bear comes to the West: The Russian agenda in Latin America." Global Americans, 20 Mar. 2019, https://theglobalamericans.org/2019/03/the-bear-comes-to-the-west-the-russian-agenda-in-latin-america/.

161 Courtney, William. "In Venezuela, a Potential U.S.-Russian Crisis?" Rand Corporation, 8 Jan. 2019, https://www.rand.org/blog/2019/01/in-venezuela-a-potential-us-russian-crisis.html

162 O'Connor, Tom. "Cold War in the West: Russia Comes to Latin America As U.S. Relations Fail." Newsweek, 16 Jan. 2019, https://www.newsweek.com/cold-war-west-russia-latin-america-us-relations-1264398

163 Chaguaceda, Armando. "The bear comes to the West: The Russian agenda in Latin America." Global Americans, 20 Mar. 2019, https://theglobalamericans.org/2019/03/the-bear-comes-to-the-west-the-russian-agenda-in-latin-america/.

key economic ends, for Russia, economic relationships serve political ends. Russia is particularly interested in the African energy sector, having invested significant sums in Algeria's oil and gas industry. Moscow has also made energy investments in Libya, Ghana, Nigeria, Ivory Coast, and Egypt.[164]

Russia has expanded its formal military agreements with many African nations, including Guinea, Burkina Faso, Burundi, and Madagascar. Like China—and unlike the U.S.—Russia imposes few standards for arms sales and defense agreements. Moscow's "no-strings-attached" approach suits nations with dubious human rights records or authoritarian regimes that have been isolated by the U.S. and its allies.

An epicenter of Russian military investment in the region is The Central African Republic, where Russia has stationed a peacekeeping force. Moscow views the CAR as strategically vital because of its location in the middle of the continent, where it stands as a kind of buffer between Africa's Muslim north and Christian south. Like many other African countries, the CAR is resource rich, especially in minerals.[165]

A private Russian defense contractor, the Wagner Group, has played a key role in training over 1,000 troops in the Central African Republic. The Wagner Group formerly trained pro-Russian separatist soldiers in the Ukrainian crisis, and the

---

164   Besenyő, János. "Russia is vying to offer African countries a credible alternative to the US and China." Quartz Africa, 4 June 2019, https://qz.com/africa/1635395/russia-keen-to-offer-alternative-to-us-and-china-in-africa/

165   Harding, Luke, and Burke, Jason. "Leaked documents reveal Russian effort to exert influence in Africa." The Guardian, 11 June 2019, https://www.theguardian.com/world/2019/jun/11/leaked-documents-reveal-russian-effort-to-exert-influence-in-africa.

U.S. Treasury Department later sanctioned it for violation of Ukrainian sovereignty. The company is run by a former Russian intelligence officer and close Putin associate.

All in all, compared with Chinese involvement on the continent, the Russian presence looks modest. But there are signs of telltale Russian ambition—and machination—that indicate that Moscow might just be getting started. A report in *The Guardian* described how Yevgeny Prigozhin, a Russian businessman and friend of Putin's, is heading up Russia's campaign to expand its influence in Africa. Leaked documents reveal that Russia is targeting as many as 13 countries across the continent. The documents make clear that Russia's goals in Africa are to "strong arm" the U.S., U.K., and France out of the region and to stymie any "pro-western" uprisings.

Janos Besenyo, a professor at Obuda University in Hungary, argues that Russia's primary goal in Africa is political. As the West rallies against Russia aggression, and as China expands its influence, Putin sees Africa as a place where Russia can develop relationships and project power. And Besenyo notes that, while the U.S. and China remain the key players in Africa, the Russian model has appeal for Africans, since "Russia offers a strategic alternative to America's global hegemony, China's economic diplomacy, and the lingering influence of Africa's former colonial masters."[166]

---

166   Besenyő, János. "Russia is vying to offer African countries a credible alternative to the US and China." Quartz Africa, 4 June 2019, https://qz.com/africa/1635395/russia-keen-to-offer-alternative-to-us-and-china-in-africa/

Adversaries

Economically, there is no avoiding the fact that the United States and China are adversaries—if for no other reason than that, for too long, the Chinese have been getting away with manipulative, illegal, and exploitative trade practices, from stealing intellectual property to requiring American trade partners to make their technological knowhow available to Chinese firms. President Trump has commendably confronted China on these practices. While I generally take a dim view of tariffs and protectionism, I believe that Trump is pursuing his current trade war with Beijing with a close eye on the national interest, and that he sees China, rightly, as a threat to American interests economically and militarily. In this sense, then, if not on the specifics of Trump's trade policy—which, in my view, will succeed in hurting China but will also hurt the U.S.—I applaud the president's explicit calling out of Beijing for its myriad offenses.

Even before the coronavirus, a confrontation with China economically was inevitable—now, it is imminent. Gordon Chang, a formidable observer of Asian politics, takes a more sweeping view: he believes that the United States should "break" with China, economically. "Why should America sign a trade agreement with a country that does not believe in trade?" he asks. America should "deny Beijing resources by, among other things, no longer supporting its economy," he argues, pointing out that "without sufficient resources, the multi-decade Soviet challenge failed, and without sufficient resources, China's would as well."

While I don't find Chang's prescription practical or even feasible, I do concur with his diagnosis and with his assessment that a much tougher American posture is essential. To that end, it is worth summarizing his views.

As Chang sees it, China's economic belligerence and aggression are the fruits of four decades of American engagement, ever since the opening to China made by the Nixon administration. Not even China's depredations against its own people in 1989, with the Tiananmen Square massacres, Chang writes, persuaded the United States to take a tougher line—on the contrary, as he points out, the administration of George H. W. Bush worked to lessen sanctions against Beijing after those incidents. Trade and globalization won the day for multiple American administrations. And, courtesy of the Clinton administration, China entered the World Trade Organization.

All this engagement and conciliation, Chang argues, has created an "uncontrollable Frankenstein." American policy-makers need to break from "fundamentally misconceived views of the nature of Chinese Communism" and stop over-optimistic assessments of China's economic and social trajectory. China has shown that it is becoming incapable, or unwilling, to participate fairly in international affairs, and the U.S. needs to confront this. Disengagement would not be painless, Chang concedes—and in fact, Americans are feeling some pain in the current tariff war, though a full disengagement would be much more difficult.

Disengagement would undoubtedly impose burdens on the American economy and moving supply chains back to domestic locations would be disruptive, but Chang believes it is possible. "Most companies can adjust quickly, shifting production in some cases in a matter of months," he writes. Disengagement would also, among other things, help stop the flow of stolen

American intellectual property to Chinese companies—which amounts to hundreds of billions each year. Chang believes that "even if Trump wanted to save China, Beijing cannot be saved. The Chinese state, for various reasons, cannot sustain a trade relationship with America," in part because its state monopolies simply won't allow for promised American involvement. And so, Chang argues that the United States aggressively disengage from China. Doing so would starve Beijing of resources and, because of China's precarious position, result in a breakdown similar to that suffered by the Soviet Union in the late 1980s.

I support this goal—bringing China's Communists to a Soviet-like demise would be an advance for humanity—but not the means. While it's true, as Chang argues, that the engagement policy has sidelined human rights for decades in the name of trade, non-engagement simply isn't the answer, any more than it was during America's Cold War with the Soviet Union. The United States is too entangled in Chinese affairs to simply "pull away," but the Trump administration's explicit confrontation with Beijing represents the first time that China has truly been called out internationally. I support more effective ways of doing that than crude trade wars. If nothing else, Trump has made it clear, going forward, that we can't go back to the status quo ante on trade with Beijing.

Of course, the American posture toward China cannot be limited to economic or even military responses. There is also the realm of diplomatic and rhetorical confrontation, a realm in which post-Cold War American policymakers have fared poorly, both in terms of speaking honestly about America's adversaries and in advocating for American principles around the world. I think that Bradley A. Thayer and Lianchao Han, writing in *The Guardian*, are correct that the United States should regard China as a "hostile, revolutionary power."[167] Thayer and Han point to a troubling July 2019 white paper in which the Chinese Communists projected Chinese power in the context of a "community with a shared future for mankind." As Thayer and Han rightly note, the Chinese tend to conflate the future of mankind with the future of China. Any "shared future" in the Chinese vision "is certain to be dystopian," and "one in which the rest of the world adapts to serve the interests of Beijing… less free, less diverse, and far more oppressive than the present one."

Thus it is more essential than ever that the United States make the case for democracy—for open political systems, for free markets, for free movement and political participation of all people, for religious liberty, for ethnic and social tolerance, for a society based on free enterprise, free endeavor, and freedom of conscience. No doubt, Donald Trump is an imperfect vessel for bearing these arguments—to say the least—but it has fallen to his administration to confront Beijing at this crucial juncture in international economic and political history. For all his flaws, he has opened the battle, and for this, I commend him. His bluster and erratic behavior aside, Trump has isolated a core truth: contrary to popular belief, China is not our friend. The CCP poses a legitimate threat to American power and stability and must be treated as such. Trump's current attitude toward China, while erratic, does represent an advance over the

---

167 Thayer, Bradley A., and Han, Lianchao. "America should view China as a hostile, revolutionary power." The Spectator, 9 Aug. 2019, https://spectator.us/america-china-hostile-revolutionary-power/

policies of past administrations, because the only language that the Chinese Communists truly understand—and respect—is that of power and force.

We can hardly afford to take a less stringent stance when it comes to Moscow. Let us remember some of the moves that Russia has made internationally over the last half decade—particularly in Ukraine, Syria, and, in the United States' backyard, Venezuela. In Ukraine, Moscow's forced annexation of Crimea in 2014 was one of the baldest moves of territorial aggression since the end of World War II, and it made clear to the world that Putin's regime has no intention of playing by the rules of the postwar international order. Tensions have continued to deepen: in late 2018, a Russian coast guard vessel rammed a Ukrainian navy tugboat in the Sea of Azov. Shortly afterward, Russian forces captured the tugboat and two other Ukrainian vessels, wounding six Ukrainian crew members. As John E. Herbst, director of the Atlantic Council's Eurasia Center, put it, Moscow's aggression is "designed to pressure Ukraine to pursue national security and economic policies subordinate to Kremlin interests."[168]

We need a lot more from President Trump in this regard. When the incident occurred, Trump's condemnation was weak, at best. "Not happy about it at all," he said, adding, "we do not like what's happening either way. And hopefully it will get straightened out." He seemed more interested in slamming NATO allies on his old theme, burden-sharing in the alliance. It sent a poor signal to the world regarding U.S. resolve against

---

168   Kumar Sen, Ashish. "The growing Russian challenge and what should be done about it." New Atlanticist, 3 May 2019, https://www.atlanticcouncil.org/blogs/new-atlanticist/the-growing-russian-challenge-and-what-should-be-done-about-it

Russian aggression in Ukraine. I agree with senators such as Bob Menendez that Trump needs to get much tougher on Russia in Ukraine, including expanding NATO exercises in the Black Sea and fortifying the security aid that we're sending Ukraine, including more lethal aid and weaponry. And the U.S. should not just persist in its sanctions regime against Moscow—we should also strengthen it.

In Syria, Russia has supplied weapons, troops, and military contractors to prop up the Assad regime, while going to bat for Assad at the United Nations. As I have written elsewhere, the United States' willingness to concede the Syrian struggle to Putin has resulted in a major new foothold for Moscow in the Middle East. Moving forward, the Trump administration should recommit itself to keeping eastern Syria free of ISIS—and, over the long term, continue to foster the development of anti-Assad alternatives in this troubled nation, site of one of the bloodiest civil wars of modern times.

Finally, it is not nearly well enough known in the United States how deeply Russia has involved itself, and allied itself with, Venezuela. Putin continues to back Nicolás Maduro, even as the United States has (effectively) backed a coup by interim (or acting) president Juan Guaidó. Russia sees Guaidó's regime as an "illegal attempt to seize power backed by the United States" and pledges to do "everything required" to support Maduro.[169] In March 2019, two Russian military aircraft carrying almost 100 military advisors and troops arrived in Caracas.

------

169 "Russian military planes land near Caracas." BBC, 25 Mar. 2019, https://www.bbc.com/news/world-latin-america-47688711

It is obvious what Venezuela's appeal is to Putin: it allows Russia to maintain a beachhead in the Americas—and Venezuela, with its anti-American politics and policies, is a key Putin ally in countering U.S. influence. The destitute nation is also a key oil market for Moscow.

I applaud Trump for saying, in March 2019, that Russia had to "get out" of Venezuela. Trump said then that all options were open for carrying out this directive, though Russia remains there, for now. It's time to make the words count: The United States should commit fully to the removal of Russian troops from Venezuela.

CHAPTER EIGHT

The Cyber, Intelligence, and Propaganda Cold War

IN JUNE 2019, THE *New York Times* PUBLISHED AN ASTOUND-ing report: The United States, it had found, had begun hacking Russia's electric power grid, deploying computer code and other cyber tools as a warning to Russia and Vladimir Putin of how the U.S. could punish him for his own continued cyber-attacks. The incursions were intended as a kind of deterrent, a hope on the part of Homeland Security and intelligence officials that the American actions might give Putin a clear idea of what he risks by letting Russia continue to insert malware into the networks of critical American infrastructure such as water systems, power plants, and energy pipelines. At the same time, of course, the American action carries its own risk: that it may escalate the cyber Cold War going on between Washington and Moscow. Like the nuclear codes, cyber "implants," once placed in the systems of adversary nations, can be turned on—and initiate shutdowns and other havoc. The worry is that Moscow and Washington are moving toward such brinkmanship, and that one day, a chain of events might be set in motion carrying major consequences.

Cyberwarfare has rapidly moved to take a central place in warfare planning for major nations. The U.S. Cyber Command was inaugurated in 2009. But as many critics warn, cyberwar is even less susceptible to political control than traditional forms of war-making, which also operate under a substantial degree of necessary secrecy. Cyber war takes secrecy to a new level: President Trump has even signed a classified directive giving Cyber Command the flexibility to launch operations autonomously, without prior presidential approval. That worries many.

And yet, clearly Washington had to do something to push back on the incredibly aggressive moves Russia has made in cyberspace over the years, moves that threaten not just systems dysfunction, but political instability.

The same goes for China, which poses a cyberthreat different in its particulars but arguably greater in magnitude and potential. As I've noted earlier, when describing China's role in stoking panic in the United States in March 2020, Beijing's capabilities in this regard are growing more sophisticated. In fact, while Russia's incursions have so far generated much more news and had more political ramifications—including the impeachment of President Trump—it is China that has been identified by U.S. intelligence officials as the leading "counter-intelligence threat" to the United States.

With highly advanced ability to manipulate data, to penetrate highly secure networks, and even to infiltrate U.S. election systems, Russia and China are the world's top cyberwarfare players. The U.S. intelligence community's 2019 Worldwide Threat Assessment maintains that the two "pose the greatest

espionage and cyber-attack threats" to American national security.[170] It's a judgment that by now is regarded as self-evident.

Moscow's Ongoing Offensive

Russia is regularly and intensely active with cyber operations
in what it calls its "near abroad," and no country has borne the
weight of Russian cyber activity more than Ukraine. Since the
Russian seizure of Crimea in 2014, Moscow has used Ukraine
as a virtual training ground for its cyber capabilities, with persistent attacks on its electrical grid and other systems, along
with economic disruptions. In 2015, a Russian hacking group
called Black Energy perpetrated a cyber-attack in Ukraine that
caused power blackouts for 225,000 people. Moscow has also
heavily attacked the Ukraine electoral system, sowing doubt in
the minds of voters about the legitimacy of the nation's electoral
outcomes.

The Russians have long menaced Georgia, as well, with
cyber attacks and cyber bullying. Ever since the short war between the two countries in 2008, Moscow has never let Georgia
rest easy. In 2019, Georgia, backed by the United States and the
U.K., accused Russia of perpetrating a massive cyber-attack on
thousands of government and private websites, with the result
that at least two major television stations in the country were
unable to broadcast for a time. It's all part of a fundamental tool
of Russian war-making called "hybrid warfare," which incor-
porates cyber hacking, disinformation campaigns, and small-

------

170 "Worldwide Threat Assessment of the U.S. Intelligence Community," 29 Jan.
2019, https://www.dni.gov/files/ODNI/documents/2019-ATA-SFR---SSCI.pdf

scale paramilitary activity to achieve, in stealthy fashion, goals pursued in earlier eras by the use of traditional military force.

The general pattern of Russian cyber activity remains largely focused on a broad goal of shaping public attitudes. "If you look at the Russians, they're primarily interested in influence operations," says former Air Force general Cedric Leighton. "What you saw in the 2016 election is a classic influence operation, but what's really key about this is that in a classic influence operation, you don't have to physically manipulate anything... you are getting into people's heads."[171]

And "getting into people's heads" certainly describes Russian efforts to disrupt the 2016 United States presidential election. The CIA, FBI, and NSA all express "high confidence" that the U.S. was a victim of a multifaceted planned Russian influence campaign, whose aim was to damage the reputation of Hilary Clinton and to disrupt the democratic process. Russia influenced the election on three main fronts: online propaganda, political hacks, and the targeting of state election systems.[172]

Most famously, of course, the Russians attacked the Clinton campaign and the Democratic National Committee. In March 2016, a Russian hacker sent John Podesta's assistant a spearphish email, which was answered. This gave the Russians access to Podesta's email account, which allowed them to collect passwords of other campaign staffers. By July 14, WikiLeaks

---

171   Sussman, Bruce. "Cyber Attack Motivations: Russia vs. China." Secure World, 3 June 2019, https://www.secureworldexpo.com/industry-news/why-russia-hacks-why-china-hacks

172   Masters, Jonathan. "Russia, Trump, and the 2016 U.S. Election." Council on Foreign Relations, 26 Feb. 2018, https://www.cfr.org/backgrounder/russia-trump-and-2016-us-election

had received an email from a Russian unit that contained an "encrypted file with instructions on accessing an online archive of leaked DNC documents." On July 22, WikiLeaks published the DNC documents, totaling about 20,000 emails and other documents.[173] The DNC email scandal was born.

Russians also hacked the Democratic Congressional Campaign Committee network, installing malware onto at least ten computers that could take screenshots and follow keystrokes. Then, they gained access to the DNC server and installed malware onto those computers. The information was released under the name Guccifer 2.0 as well as on the website DCLeaks. com—both entities controlled by Russian hackers.[174]

In July 2018, Robert Mueller's indictments revealed political motives behind the date of the release of the DCCC, DNC, and Clinton emails. Correspondence between WikiLeaks and Russian hackers showed that the emails were released purposefully before the Democratic National Convention to stir up trouble between the Clinton and Bernie Sanders campaigns—the hacked DNC emails contained messages of high-ranking Democrats belittling Sanders and making clear that they wanted the party to coalesce behind Clinton. The goal of sowing Democratic dissension was achieved: Sanders's appeals at the convention to support Hillary were booed by his supporters in the hall.

---

173 Chang, Alvin. "How Russian hackers stole information from Democrats, in 3 simple diagrams." Vox, 16 Jul. 2018https://www.vox.com/policy-and-poli-tics/2018/7/16/17575940/russian-election-hack-democrats-trump-putin-diagram

174 Nilson, Ella. "The Mueller indictments reveal the timing of the DNC leak was intentional." Vox, 13 Jul. 2018, https://www.vox.com/2018/7/13/17569030/mueller-in-dictments-russia-hackers-bernie-sanders-hillary-clinton-democratic-national-convention

Russian activity went beyond national politics. The Department of Homeland Security revealed that Russian hackers targeted vulnerabilities and tried to hack election-related computer systems in 21 states.[175] In Arizona and Illinois, voter-registration systems were hacked by Russians in summer 2016. In Arizona, Secretary of State Michele Reagan shut down the state's voting systems temporarily. The Mueller report also revealed that the Russians used a spear-phishing email to gain access to a network of "at least one Florida county government."[176] The Russian military intelligence unit, the G.R.U., sent emails containing Trojan viruses to 120 election officials in Florida.

Likewise, Russian attacks have hit American public systems. On the last day of 2016, Russian code was discovered in the systems of a Vermont public utility. The Russians did not activate the codes to perpetrate an attack, but its presence made clear their success at penetrating American firewalls. The incursion may have simply been a Russian dry run, though that should console no one. As a Homeland Security report later summarized, the Russian activity was "part of an ongoing campaign of cyber-enabled operations directed at the U.S. government and

---

175   Zapotosky, Matt, and Demirjian, Karoun. "Homeland Security official: Russian government actors tried to hack election systems in 21 states." Washington Post, 21 June 2017,   https://www.washingtonpost.com/world/national-security/homeland-security-official-russian-government-actors-potentially-tried-to-hack-election-systems-in-21-states/2017/06/21/33bf31d4-5686-11e7-ba90-f5875b7d1876_story.html?utm_term=.331639728c23

176   Robles, Frances. "Russian Hackers Were 'In a Position' to Alter Florida Voter Rolls, Rubio Confirms." New York Times, 26 Apr. 2019, https://www.nytimes.com/2019/04/26/us/florida-russia-hacking-election.html

its citizens. These cyber operations have included spear phishing campaigns targeting government organizations, critical infrastructure entities, think tanks, universities, political organizations, and corporations leading to the theft of information."[177]

In March 2017, customers of All-Ways Excavating USA, a 15-person construction firm in Oregon, started receiving suspicious emails asking them to sign an agreement. They started calling the company for an explanation; an employee there knew nothing about it. Then he was contacted by Homeland Security, which let him know that his systems had been hacked. The construction firm works with utilities and government agencies, and the Russian hackers were trying to hack the power grid by way of All-Ways' systems.

The attack worked through an email to customers, which was intended to drive them to a website run by the hackers. The email drives the customers to "download the file directly" when they clicked—when they did, nothing happened, at least on their end. But those clicks were what the hackers needed to make their penetrations.

If this sounds small bore, don't be deceived. Consider how it rippled out, as the *Wall Street Journal* reported:

> The hackers planted malware on sites of online publications frequently read by utility engineers. They sent out fake résumés with tainted attachments, pretending to be job seekers. Once they had computer-network credentials, they slipped through hidden portals used by

---

177 "GRIZZLY STEPPE – Russian Malicious Cyber Activity." Federal Bureau of Investigation, 29 Dec. 2016, https://www.us-cert.gov/sites/default/files/publications/JAR_16-20296A_GRIZZLY%20STEPPE-2016-1229.pdf

utility technicians, in some cases getting into computer systems that monitor and control electricity flows…

One company that got one of the bogus emails was a small professional-services firm in Corvallis, Ore. That July, FBI agents showed up there, telling employees their system had been compromised in a "widespread campaign" targeting energy companies, according to the company owner…

In June 2017, the hackers used the Corvallis company's systems to go hunting. Over the next month, they accessed the Oregon company's network dozens of times from computers with IP addresses registered in countries including Turkey, France and the Netherlands, targeting at least six energy firms.[178]

The strategy: avoid a direct attack on the core system and go after its many subsidiary points—its hundreds of contractors and subcontractors, who would not have had any reason to fear being targeted. Break into one of those, the thinking went, and you could start working your way up the chain. The Russians may have succeeded in using this strategy to breach two dozen utility systems.[179]

We can be sure that more such attempts lie ahead, but when the Russians aren't busy hacking into systems, they are working assiduously and with a high degree of effectiveness to create and disseminate misinformation and the now-infamous commod-

---

178   Smith, Rebecca, and Barry, Rob. "America's Electric Grid Has a Vulnerable Back Door—and Russia Walked Through It." Wall Street Journal, 10 Jan. 2019,   https://www.wsj.com/articles/americas-electric-grid-has-a-vulnerable-back-doorand-russia-walked-through-it-11547137112

179   Ibid.

ity known as "fake news." Moscow's formidable trolling group, the Internet Research Agency (IRA), based in St. Petersburg, is undoubtedly tied to the Kremlin. In 2018 Mueller indicted 13 individuals linked to the group on the grounds that "the IRA was engaged in 'information warfare' to 'sow discord' during the 2016 election through its use of social-media accounts falsely claiming to be ordinary Americans."[180] The main goal of the organization was to rack up as much anti-Clinton propaganda as possible. The trolls reportedly took English classes and learned about American holidays to seem as American as possible.[181] The troll farm was funded by Russian oligarch and Putin ally Yevgeny Prigozhin.[182] The trollers masked themselves as fake activist groups, like "Secured Borders" and "Blacktivist," and notably "Don't Shoot Us," a group that posed as a part of the Black Lives Matter movement and used most major social media platforms, including Pokémon Go.[183] The idea, again, was to sow discord.

Millions saw or interacted with the Russian trollers' posts and accounts. Facebook testified that about 126 million Facebook users had seen Russian-linked content. Twitter found more than 3,800 accounts linked to the Internet Research Agency.

---

180   Feldman, Brian. "Mueller Indicts Employees of Russian 'Troll Farm' Internet Research Agency." New York, 16 Feb. 2018, http://nymag.com/intelligencer/2018/02/mueller-indicts-internet-research-agency-and-employees.html.

181   Kirby, Jen. "What to know about the Russian troll factory listed in Mueller's indictment." Vox, 16 Feb. 2018, https://www.vox.com/2018/2/16/17020974/mueller-indictment-internet-research-agency

182   Kirby, Jen. "The US launched a cyberattack on a Russian troll factory during the 2018 midterms." Vox, 26 Feb. 2019, https://www.vox.com/2019/2/26/18241654/us-cyberattack-internet-research-agency-russia-2018-elections

183   O'Sullivan, Donnie, and Byers, Dylan. "Even Pokémon Go used by extensive Russian-linked meddling effort." CNNMoney, 13 Oct. 2017 https://money.cnn.com/2017/10/12/media/dont-shoot-us-russia-pokemon-go/index.html

Finally, there is the effective work of Russian media outlets, especially the website and radio broadcaster Sputnik and television network Russia Today (RT), to shape perceptions. It has become very difficult to disaggregate the quantity of news appearing online from what portion of it might be planted or at least affected by Russian influencers—the 2016 election makes this clear. We should expect more of the same in the 2020 election—and, almost certainly, new and previously unanticipated methods and tactics.

Putin's goal

The fundamental thing to remember about Russia's cyber-war on the United States is this: leaving aside the particulars about individual hacking episodes, about which targets are most vulnerable, and about what we need to do to protect our systems—all worthy and important questions—we must realize that Putin's broader goal extends beyond any individual achievement of specific attacks. It involves nothing less than the delegitimization of American institutions, an erosion of faith in American democratic processes, and in the fostering of a mounting cynicism among the American people about the truthfulness or reliability of almost *anything* they are told by their governments, institutions, and media. This is the true Russian objective. Yes, Putin wouldn't mind stealing state secrets, and yes, he's interested—as the Russian incursions suggest—in exploiting all of our systemic vulnerabilities, but more than anything else he wants to demoralize the American people by setting us against one another and fostering the kind of environment that we increasingly live in: one in which objective truth no longer exists, in which one chooses one's own news to believe, on the premise that everyone is lying, anyway.

To the extent that Putin has been successful in fostering this attitude—and in my view, he has been staggeringly successful—this marks a remarkable assault on American stability, social cohesion, and political functioning. I've written it before and I will say it here again: whether Putin wanted Donald Trump to win the 2016 election or not is beside the point. My guess is that yes, he did want Trump to win—but Trump really wasn't the issue. What matters is that, even had Hillary Clinton won in 2016, Putin would have succeeded in rendering the election result essentially illegitimate to whichever side lost. Does anyone believe that Trump supporters would have been any less conspiracy minded than Hillary supporters have been, post-election, in pointing fingers and suggesting dark plots? We have become a nation of rabid partisans, with a substantial dose of conspiratorialism thrown in; we believe, on both sides of the partisan divide, that our American system is no longer trustworthy, admirable, even legitimate.

If you don't see Vladimir Putin's hand in this outcome, you're not paying attention.

The Threat from Beijing

Meanwhile, China in the words of FBI director Christopher Wray, is "more challenging, more comprehensive and more concerning than any counter-intelligence threat" that the United States faces today—including Russia.[184] At a February 2020

---

184   Hoke, Zlatica. "FBI Director: China Poses Biggest Counterintelligence Threat to US." VOA News,   24 July, 2019, https://www.voanews.com/episode/fbi-director-china-poses-biggest-counterintelligence-threat-us-3967386

talk for the Center for Strategic and International Studies, Wray said that his bureau had "about 1,000 investigations involving China's attempted theft of US-based technology in all 56 of our field offices and spanning just about every industry sector."[185]

China's rise to such stature should not be surprising for those who know its post-Cold War history. The prowess in technological spying dates back to the People's Republic's founding of the China Ministry of State Security in 1983, the equivalent of the American CIA. According to an important book, *Chinese Communist Espionage*, by Peter Mattis and Matthew Brazil, China's long-running weakness in using human assets for spying abroad may have been the impetus for its development of sophisticated electronic espionage.

Still, while the cyber capabilities are a more recent development, it's important to remember that Beijing has been in the spying business for a long time—and it has had success recruiting American turncoats for a long time, even as far back as the Cold War's earliest days.

"The ignominious list of Americans, both of Chinese descent and otherwise, who have sold national or corporate secrets to China, or attempted to do so, is enough to raise questions about how much of China's military and economic rise could have been achieved without espionage," writes Michael Auslin, a China expert.

Auslin lays out some examples:

---

185 "China theft of technology is biggest law enforcement threat to US, FBI says." The Guardian, 6 Feb. 2020, https://www.theguardian.com/world/2020/feb/06/china-technology-theft-fbi-biggest-threat

In October 2018, a high-ranking MSS officer was arrested in Belgium and extradited to the United States,
charged with economic espionage at U.S. aerospace
firms, while in September 2019 a Chinese-born natural-
ized U.S. citizen, Edward Peng, was arrested by the FBI
after a "double cross" operation revealed he was acting
as a courier for the MSS. A Chinese military officer was
indicted for lying on her visa application to study at an
advanced physics laboratory at Boston University, with
instructions to covertly gather information on leading
U.S. scientists.[186]

A Chinese spy was even apprehended trying to sneak his
way into Mar-a-Lago, President Trump's Florida resort. Chinese spies see little reason to fear America, it seems.

And why should they? Beijing has, after all, committed the
biggest cybercrime of this young century: its theft, in 2014, of 22
million personnel files from the U.S. government. The Chinese
made off with a "treasure trove of information about everybody
who has worked for, tried to work for, or works for the United
States government," said then FBI director James Comey. It represented, he said, "a very big deal from a national security… and
counterintelligence perspective."[187] The U.S. Worldwide Threat
Assessment maintains that China has the capability to "launch
cyber attacks that cause localized, temporary disruptive effects

------

186   Auslin, Michael. "'Chinese Communist Espionage' Review: Spycraft as State-
craft." Wall Street Journal, 1 Mar. 2020, https://www.wsj.com/articles/chinese-com-
munist-espionage-review-spycraft-as-statecraft-11583100597

187   Buchanan, Patrick J. "China, Not Russia, the Greater Threat." Rasmussen
Reports, 13 Aug. 2019, http://www.rasmussenreports.com/public_content/political_
commentary/commentary_by_pat_buchanan/china_not_russia_the_greater_threat

on critical infrastructure—such as disruption of a natural gas pipeline for days to weeks—in the United States."[188]

The Chinese are expert at stealing intellectual property. As assistant attorney general John Demers told the Senate Judiciary Committee, the Chinese economic policy is to "rob, replicate, and replace." He goes on: "The playbook is simple. Rob the American company of its intellectual property. Replicate the technology. And replace the American company in the Chinese market and one day in the global market."[189]

During Barack Obama's second term in the White House, cyber espionage by the Chinese had become a major issue for American companies. Obama considered imposing sanctions on China.[190] During Xi's state visit in September 2015, he and Obama finalized an agreement that cracked down on cybersecurity attacks. From the time the deal was created until Trump took office, the number of commercial hacks significantly declined. According to Crowdstrike, a cybersecurity company, the hacks might have "plummeted as much as 90 percent in the months after the agreement."[191]Since Trump has taken office, though, commercial theft has increased, according to many of-

------

188 "Worldwide Threat Assessment of the U.S. Intelligence Community," 29 Jan. 2019, https://www.dni.gov/files/ODNI/documents/2019-ATA-SFR---SSCI.pdf

189 Townsend, Kevin. "The United States and China - A Different Kind of Cyberwar." Security Week, 7 Jan. 2019,   https://www.securityweek.com/united-states-and-china-different-kind-cyberwar

190 Sevastopulo, Demetri, and Dyer, Geoff. "Obama and Xi in deal on cyber espionage." Financial Times, 25 Sep. 2015,   https://www.ft.com/content/0dbcab36-63be-11e5-a28b-50226830d644

191 "China 'has taken the gloves off' in thefts of technology secrets." South China Morning Post, 19 Nov. 2018, https://www.scmp.com/news/world/united-states-canada/article/2173843/china-has-taken-gloves-its-thefts-us-technology

ficials and field experts. It's hard to gauge if the theft is occurring at the same rate as before the 2015 deal.[192]

Before 2014, about 90% of Chinese cyber espionage came from the infamous Unit 61398 of the People's Liberation Army, based in Shanghai. Its main focus: collecting "political, economic and military related intelligence."[193] But Unit 61398 got caught in the crosshairs of U.S. intelligence—which indicted some of its operatives—and that, along with the Xi/Obama pact, brought its days as a cyber-intelligence all-star team to an end. Now, in the Trump years, China has regenerated these capacities with what the *New York Times* calls "stealthier operatives in the country's intelligence agencies."[194]

Those stealthier operatives have become positively ingenious at hacking American targets. The U.S. Navy, in an internal review, concluded that Chinese hackers had stolen critical national security secrets in recent years, to the extent that the thefts "threaten the U.S.'s standing as the world's top military power."[195] The report described how the Navy was scrambling

---

192 "China 'has taken the gloves off' in thefts of technology secrets." South China Morning Post, 19 Nov. 2018, https://www.scmp.com/news/world/united-states-canada/article/2173843/china-has-taken-gloves-its-thefts-us-technology

193 Sanger, David E., Barboza, David, and Perlroth, Nicole. "Chinese Army Unit Is Seen as Tied to Hacking Against U.S." New York Times, 19 Feb. 2013, https://www.nytimes.com/2013/02/19/technology/chinas-army-is-seen-as-tied-to-hacking-against-us.html?module=inline

194 Sanger, David E., and Myers, Steven Lee. "After a Hiatus, China Accelerates Cyberspying Efforts to Obtain U.S. Technology." New York Times, 29 Nov. 2018, https://www.nytimes.com/2018/11/29/us/politics/china-trump-cyberespionage.html

195 Lubold, Gordon, and Volz, Dustin. "Navy, Industry Partners Are 'Under Cyber Siege' by Chinese Hackers, Review Asserts." Wall Street Journal, 12 Mar. 2019, https://www.wsj.com/articles/navy-industry-partners-are-under-cyber-siege-review-asserts-11552415553

to respond effectively to the incursions—and, so far at least, not offering an optimistic assessment of their success. The thefts have included highly classified information regarding military technology. And, as bad as the thefts have been, the report also makes clear that Navy officials and intelligence analysts are far from clear in the extent of the attacks and the damage, because of the complexity and difficulty of tracking all the incursions.

China's hackers are even good at what might be called counter-hacking—that is, obtaining American cyberwarfare tools and putting them to their own uses. In 2016, for example, Chinese intelligence agents acquired hacking tools from the National Security Agency and used them against American allies and private companies in Europe and Asia, according to a report in the *New York Times*. The Chinese hackers used these tools to carry out cyber-attacks against a broad range of organizations and computer networks in Belgium, Luxembourg, Vietnam, the Philippines, and Hong Kong. The Chinese were able to capture the tools—really, the code for the tools—from an NSA attack on their own computers, what the *Times* described as something "like a gunslinger who grabs an enemy's rifle and starts blasting away."[196]

It is one thing for the United States to see its systems of government or private business be targeted by cyber-attackers, whether from Beijing or Moscow. It is another when the steps the United States takes to protect itself—which, in part, rely on proactive cyber-attacks of its own—can be turned against

---

196   Perlroth, Nicole, Sanger, David E., and Shane, Scott. "How Chinese Spies Got the N.S.A.'s Hacking Tools, and Used Them for Attacks." New York Times, 6 May 2019, https://www.nytimes.com/2019/05/06/us/politics/china-hacking-cyber.html

it by a savvy enemy. Indeed, this experience and others like it, according to the *Times* report, have "touched off a debate within the intelligence community over whether the United States should continue to develop some of the world's most high-tech, stealthy cyberweapons if it is unable to keep them under lock and key."

The report, based on research by the cybersecurity firm Symantec, found that the attack was perpetrated by a hacking group considered to be among the most dangerous and savvy in China—what Symantec calls the Buckeye group, a code name for what is regarded by the U.S. government as a Chinese Ministry of State Security contractor operating out of Guangzhou.

This is far from the first time that such a thing has happened. Over the past decade, American intelligence's cyber tools have repeatedly fallen into the wrong hands. Just why, exactly, the Chinese have not turned these weapons against the United States directly, in the form of an overt cyber-attack, is not entirely clear. Perhaps they don't wish to take that risk; Symantec speculated that the Chinese "might assume Americans have developed defenses against their own weapons, and they might not want to reveal to the United States that they had stolen American tools." But what a sobering reminder of American vulnerabilities, to have to rely on our adversaries' reluctance, not our own capabilities.

China's business threat

Another concern is the Chinese communications technology giant Huawei, which sells consumer electronics like smartphones, tablets, and computers. Currently Huawei accounts for about 16% of the smartphone market.[197] Huawei is developing 5G networks—but the U.S. and Australia have banned Huawei products that can be used on 5G networks, and Canada is reviewing the situation. The United States is concerned that the company's founder, Ren Zhengfei, was a Chinese army officer. Huawei could hack into 5G networks because it has been selling equipment to build these—which means that the company could break into electric grids and cars that rely on the networks.

Verizon and AT&T ban Huawei products on their networks because of the security threat. There are no direct lines between the Chinese government and Huawei, but according to a senior international defense analyst at the RAND Corporation, "the threat is legitimate, given the murky links between Huawei and Chinese authorities. The Chinese state has the authority to demand tech companies like Huawei turn over useful information or provide access to the communications and technologies owned and sold by Huawei. Chinese authorities can use this information and access to facilitate espionage or cyber attacks over Huawei communications technologies."[198]

American companies hesitate to accuse China of stealing information because they have a big stake in the Chinese market; most cases go public only because people or companies

---

197 "Global market share held by leading smartphone vendors from 4th quarter 2009 to 1st quarter 2020." Statista, 10 Jun. 2020, https://www.statista.com/statistics/271496/global-market-share-held-by-smartphone-vendors-since-4th-quarter-2009/

198 O'Flaherty, Kate. "Huawei Security Scandal: Everything You Need to Know." Forbes, 26 Feb. 2019, https://www.forbes.com/sites/kateoflahertyuk/2019/02/26/huawei-security-scandal-everything-you-need-to-know/#7c0d6d1473a5

have been brought to court. The publicly known cases are enough to warrant serious concern. In 2018, Jizhong Chen, an Apple employee, stole information about self-driving cars. Chen worked with Xiaolang Zhang; they both took photos of confidential work. Allegedly Zhang was going to bring this information to a Chinese electric car startup, Xiaoping Motors. Both were arrested before they boarded planes to China.[199] In 2108, Sinovel Wind Group stole information about wind turbines from AMSC (American Superconductor). "Over 8,000 wind turbines—an estimated 20 percent of China's fleet—are now running on AMSC's stolen software," said Daniel Mc-Gahn, the company's CEO. The company lost $1 billion in value and had to cut 700 jobs.[200]

China's state-owned Fujian Jinhua Integrated Circuit Co., along with Taiwan's United Microelectronics Corp., stole information from Micron, a U.S. company that produces computer chips and controls about 25% of the dynamic random-access memory (DRAM) industry. Micron is worth $100 billion.[201]

---

199 Wiseman, Paul, and Liedtke, Michael. "Here are 5 cases where the U.S. says Chinese companies and workers stole American trade secrets." Chicago Tribune, 21 Feb. 2019, https://www.chicagotribune.com/business/ct-biz-us-china-trade-war-ip-theft-20190221-story.html

200 Wiseman, Paul, and Liedtke, Michael. "Here are 5 cases where the U.S. says Chinese companies and workers stole American trade secrets." Chicago Tribune, 21 Feb. 2019, https://www.chicagotribune.com/business/ct-biz-us-china-trade-war-ip-theft-20190221-story.html

201 Kelly, Makena. "China state-owned company charged with stealing US tech trade secrets." The Verge, 1 Nov. 2018, https://www.theverge.com/2018/11/1/18052784/china-chip-stolen-trade-secrets-justice-department-semiconductor

The Department of Justice valued the stolen chip at between $400 million and $8.75 billion.[202]

Teamwork

Finally, there is the matter of cyber collaboration between Russia and China, or at least mutual agreement not to impinge on one another's digital turf. The two countries made a bilateral cybersecurity deal in May 2015 described by some in the media as a kind of non-aggression pact. Indeed, the deal's two key components pledged nonaggression in cyberspace and advocacy of cyber-sovereignty. In a sense, it is a pledge not to hack against one another—even as the two countries freely hack elsewhere.

And hack elsewhere they continue to do—even, it would appear, during the coronavirus pandemic. In March 2020, as the pandemic and the resulting lockdown began to unfold in the United States, the computer systems of the Department of Health and Human Services were hacked. There was no serious damage, and the system was not brought down, but its timing was suspicious, to say the least—and government officials, without making any official declarations, suspect two likely culprits.

"It is safe to say that there are only two places in the world that could hit (the Department of Health and Human Services) the way it's been hit," one said.[203] He meant Russia and China,

---

202   Nichols, Shaun. "US charges Chinese biz, staff over DRAM chip secrets theft." The Register, 1 Nov. 2018, https://www.theregister.co.uk/2018/11/01/doj_micron_dram/

203   Cohen, Zachary, and Marquardt, Alex. 'They are trying to steal everything.' US coronavirus response hit by foreign hackers." CNN, 25 Apr. 2020, https://www.cnn.com/2020/04/25/politics/us-china-cyberattacks-coronavirus-research/index.html

of course, though in this particular case, it appears that government officials are leaning more toward China as the principal culprit. The Trump administration also alleges that Beijing has tried to steal U.S. research on the coronavirus, through hacks on pharmaceutical companies, hospitals, and research labs. The cyber war will not pause, not even for a pandemic.

CHAPTER NINE

Some Thoughts on Fighting Back

THERE IS NO EASY ROAD AHEAD FOR THE UNITED STATES. As I write, America is just four and a half months away from the 2020 presidential election—an election that promises to be among the most tumultuous in the history of the country, and one that may well even test the nation's long-running pride in conducting peaceful and orderly transfers of power. American institutions, American governance, and American social cohesion and civil order are being tested in 2020 more severely than at any time since 1968. (I have more to say about this in the Afterword.)

Yet even the internal and domestic crises that America is struggling with, as serious as they are, cannot change the reality that in a globalized world, the challenge posed by China and its partner Russia is simply not going away. Its formidability, in fact, is all the more reason (if more reason were needed) why the United States needs to get its own house in order. For years, I have written about this challenge at considerable length, including lengthy suggestions and ideas for going forward. My primary goal in writing this briefer book has been to raise the alarm about the current situation and less concerned with specific policy proposals, but what follows below is a more succinct discussion and thoughts on some key areas.

Economy

Economically, there is no avoiding the fact that the United States and China are adversaries—if for no other reason than that, for too long, the Chinese have been getting away with manipulative, illegal, and exploitative trade practices, from stealing intellectual property to requiring American trade partners to make their technological knowhow available to Chinese firms. President Trump has commendably confronted China on these practices. While I generally take a dim view of tariffs and protectionism, I believe that Trump is pursuing his current trade war with Beijing with a close eye on the national interest, and that he sees China, rightly, as a threat to American interests economically and militarily. In this sense, then, if not on the specifics of Trump's trade policy—which, in my view, will succeed in hurting China but will also hurt the U.S.—I applaud the president's explicit calling out of Beijing for its myriad offenses.

A confrontation with China economically cannot be avoided. Gordon Chang, a formidable observer of Asian politics, takes a more sweeping view: he believes that the United States should "break" with China, economically. "Why should America sign a trade agreement with a country that does not believe in trade?" he asks. America should "deny Beijing resources by, among other things, no longer supporting its economy," he argues, pointing out that "without sufficient resources, the multi-decade Soviet challenge failed, and without sufficient resources, China's would as well."[204]

This is what is known broadly as "decoupling," a step many called for in the wake of the coronavirus and the shutdowns in the United States that did so much damage to Americans economically and socially. The argument is that the virus showed, once and for all, that the United States must sever economic links with China, lest we find ourselves in the terribly vulnerable and dependent situation of March 2020, when the pandemic came to our door and we lacked the productive capacity to supply our most pressing needs, from protective medical gear to medicines.

While I don't find Chang's prescription practical or even feasible, I do concur with his diagnosis and with his assessment that a much tougher American posture is essential. To that end, it is worth summarizing his views.

As Chang sees it, China's economic belligerence and aggression are the fruits of four decades of American engagement, ever since the opening to China made by the Nixon administration. Not even China's depredations against its own people in 1989, with the Tiananmen Square massacres, Chang writes, persuaded the United States to take a tougher line—on the contrary, as he points out, the administration of George H. W. Bush worked to lessen sanctions against Beijing after those incidents. Trade and globalization won the day for multiple American

---

204   Chang, Gordon. "It's Time for America to Break with Beijing." The National Interest, 19 June 2019, https://nationalinterest.org/print/feature/its-time-america-break-beijing-63327.

administrations. And, courtesy of the Clinton administration, China entered the World Trade Organization.

All this engagement and conciliation, Chang argues, has created an "uncontrollable Frankenstein." American policy-makers need to break from "fundamentally misconceived views of the nature of Chinese Communism" and stop over-op-timistic assessments of China's economic and social trajectory. China has shown that it is becoming incapable, or unwilling, to participate fairly in international affairs, and the U.S. needs to confront this. Disengagement would not be painless, Chang concedes—and in fact, Americans are feeling some pain in the current tariff war, though a full disengagement would be much more difficult.

Disengagement would undoubtedly impose burdens on the American economy. Moving supply chains back to domestic locations would be disruptive, but Chang believes it is possi-ble. "Most companies can adjust quickly, shifting production in some cases in a matter of months," he writes. Disengagement would also, among other things, help stop the flow of stolen American intellectual property to Chinese companies—which amounts to hundreds of billions each year. Chang believes that "even if Trump wanted to save China, Beijing cannot be saved. The Chinese state, for various reasons, cannot sustain a trade relationship with America," in part because its state monopolies simply won't allow for promised American involvement.[205] And so Chang argues that the United States aggressively disengage

---

205   Chang, Gordon. "It's Time for America to Break with Beijing." The National Interest, 19 June 2019, https://nationalinterest.org/print/feature/its-time-america-break-beijing-63327.

from China. Doing so would starve Beijing of resources and, because of China's precarious position, result in a breakdown similar to that suffered by the Soviet Union in the late 1980s.

I support this goal—bringing China's Communists to a Soviet-like demise would be an advance for humanity—but not the means. While it's true, as Chang argues, that the engagement policy has sidelined human rights for decades in the name of trade, non-engagement simply isn't the answer, any more than it was during America's Cold War with the Soviet Union. The United States is too entangled in Chinese affairs to simply "pull away," but the Trump administration's explicit confrontation with Beijing represents the first time that China has truly been called out internationally. I support more effective ways of doing that than crude trade wars. If nothing else, Trump has made it clear, going forward, that we can't go back to the status quo ante on trade with Beijing.

And, fortunately, given what the United States has just been through with the coronavirus, there is now widespread support for strong concrete steps to reduce dependence on China and redefine our trade relationship—in ways that would stop short of an outright decoupling but that would nevertheless prove constructive, even decisive. For example, after the debacle of the U.S. lacking medical supplies and medicines during the pandemic, bipartisan support exists in Congress to bring more production for these things back to our shores, including pharmaceutical manufacture. Most Americans, it seems to me, were virtually unaware of how extensively the United States had let these areas become the industrial province of China. If, to borrow a much-maligned phrase, we shouldn't let a crisis go to waste, then this is certainly an area where a catastrophe as dramatic as Covid-19 has been for America ought to point us toward some major improvements in our trade policy and some restoration of domestic self-sufficiency.

I believe that we will also see greater scrutiny brought to other areas, ranging from artificial intelligence to telecom—especially the role of Huawei—and even about exchange programs involving Chinese college student and research scientists. In these areas, the issue is not American self-sufficiency but American self-protection. Chinese espionage, as I have detailed, is growing ever more sophisticated, and if we want to protect ourselves, we're going to have to ask some hard questions about even some popular programs.

Of course, the American posture toward China cannot be limited to economic or even military responses. There is also the realm of diplomatic and rhetorical confrontation, a realm in which post-Cold War American policymakers have fared poorly, both in terms of speaking honestly about America's adversaries and in advocating for American principles around the world. I think that Bradley A. Thayer and Lianchao Han, writing in *The Guardian*, are correct that the United States should regard China as "hostile, revolutionary power."[206] Thayer and Han point to a troubling July 2019 white paper in which the Chinese Communists projected Chinese power in the context of a "community with a shared future for mankind." As they rightly note, the Chinese tend to conflate the future of mankind with the future of China. Any "shared future," in the Chinese

---

206   Thayer, Bradley A., and Han, Lianchao. "America should view China as a hostile, revolutionary power." *Spectator USA*, 9 Aug. 2019, https://spectator.us/america-china-hostile-revolutionary-power/.

vision, "is certain to be dystopian," and "one in which the rest of the world adapts to serve the interests of Beijing… less free, less diverse, and far more oppressive than the present one."

Thus it is more essential than ever that the United States make the case for democracy—both at home and abroad.

What does that mean? It means open political systems; it means free markets; it means free movement and political participation of all people; it means religious and political liberty; it means racial, ethnic, religious, and social tolerance; it means a society based on free enterprise, free endeavor, and freedom of conscience.

No doubt, Donald Trump is an imperfect vessel for bearing these arguments—to say the least—but it has fallen to his administration to confront Beijing at this crucial juncture in international economic and political history. For all Trump's flaws, he has opened the battle, and for this, I commend him. His bluster and erratic behavior aside, Trump has isolated a core truth: contrary to popular belief, China is not our friend. The CCP poses a legitimate threat to American power and stability and must be treated as such. Trump's current attitude toward China, while erratic, does represent an advance over the policies of past administrations, because the only language that the Chinese Communists truly understand—and respect—is that of power and force.

◆ ◆ ◆

We can hardly afford to take a less stringent stance when it comes to Moscow. Let us remember some of the moves that Russia has made internationally over the last half decade—particularly in Ukraine, Syria, and, in the United States' backyard, Venezuela. In Ukraine, Moscow's forced annexation of Crimea in 2014 was one of the baldest moves of territorial aggression since the end of World War II, and it made clear to the world that Putin's regime has no intention of playing by the rules of the postwar international order. Tensions have continued to deepen: in late 2018, a Russian coast guard vessel rammed a Ukrainian navy tugboat in the Sea of Azov. Shortly afterward, Russian forces captured the tugboat and two other Ukrainian vessels, wounding six Ukrainian crew members. As John E. Herbst, director of the Atlantic Council's Eurasia Center, put it, Moscow's aggression is "designed to pressure Ukraine to pursue national security and economic policies subordinate to Kremlin interests."[207]

We need a lot more from President Trump in this regard. When the incident occurred, Trump's condemnation was weak, at best. "Not happy about it at all," he said, adding, "we do not like what's happening either way. And hopefully it will get straightened out." He seemed more interested in slamming NATO allies on his old theme, burden-sharing in the alliance. It sent a poor signal to the world regarding U.S. resolve against Russian aggression in Ukraine. I agree with senators such as Bob Menendez that Trump needs to get much tougher on Russia in Ukraine, including expanding NATO exercises in the Black Sea and fortifying the security aid that we're sending Ukraine, including more lethal aid and weaponry. And the U.S. should not

---

207   Sen, Ashish Kumar. "The growing Russian challenge and what should be done about it." Atlantic Council, 3 May 2019, https://www.atlanticcouncil.org/blogs/new-atlanticist/the-growing-russian-challenge-and-what-should-be-done-about-it/.

just persist in its sanctions regime against Moscow—it should also strengthen it.

In Syria, Russia has supplied weapons, troops, and military contractors to prop up the Assad regime, while going to bat for Assad at the United Nations. As I have written elsewhere, the United States' willingness to concede the Syrian struggle to Putin has resulted in a major new foothold for Moscow in the Middle East. Moving forward, the Trump administration should recommit itself to keeping eastern Syria free of ISIS— and, over the long term, continue to foster the development of anti-Assad alternatives in this troubled nation, site of one of the bloodiest civil wars of modern times.

Finally, it is not nearly well enough known in the United States how deeply Russia has involved itself, and allied itself with, Venezuela. Putin continues to back Nicolás Maduro, even as the United States has (effectively) backed a coup by interim (or acting) president Juan Guaidó. Russia sees Guaidó's regime as an "illegal attempt to seize power backed by the United States" and pledges to do "everything required" to support Maduro.[208] In March 2019, two Russian military aircraft carrying almost 100 military advisors and troops arrived in Caracas.

It is obvious what Venezuela's appeal is to Putin: it allows Russia to maintain a beachhead in the Americas—and Venezuela, with its anti-American politics and policies, is a key Putin ally in countering U.S. influence. The destitute nation is also a key oil market for Moscow.

---

208 "Russian Military Planes Land Near Caracas." BBC, 25 Mar. 2019, https://www.bbc.com/news/world-latin-america-47688711

I applaud Trump for saying, in March 2019, that Russia had to "get out" of Venezuela. Trump said then that all options were open for carrying out this directive, though Russia remains there, for now. It's time to make the words count: The United States should commit fully to the removal of Russian troops from Venezuela.

The Military Challenge

A crucial aspect of addressing the Russia/China challenge is updating the American military posture, both strategically and materially. The United States must evolve beyond what Elbridge Colby calls the "Gulf War model" of fighting rogue states and re-prepare itself so that it can take on militaries such as China's and Russia's—not in head-to-head global conflicts, but in a manner that can effectively check their aggressive actions before they occur.

Colby, a former director of the defense program at the Center for a New American Security, has written an enormously important and insightful article for *Foreign Policy* called "How to Win America's Next War." He argues that the U.S. has spent a generation on the military model of fighting rogue states, as exemplified in the Gulf War and the later Iraq War—a focus that moved us away from our previous Cold War goal of checking the moves of great-power military adversaries. Such preparation is the only way to prevent further aggression such as Russia's seizure of Crimea in 2014—an episode that illustrates Colby's thesis, and serves as an example of what he calls "fait accompli" logic, which involves an aggressor "seizing territory before the defender and its patron can react sufficiently and then making sure that the counterattack needed to eject it would be so risky, costly, and aggressive that the United States would balk at mounting it—not least because its allies might see it as unjustified and refuse to support it." This is precisely what happened in Crimea, and what will continue to happen until the United States is better able to ward off such incursions before they happen, or, early enough in their process, to undo them. Once fait accompli logic kicks in, it's too late—and Colby explains the ramifications:

> Russia and especially China are the only countries that could plausibly take over and hold the territory of Washington's allies and partners in the face of U.S. resistance. If they did so—or even if they merely convinced their neighbors that they could and then used that fear to suborn them—they could unravel U.S. alliances and shift in their favor the balances of power in Europe and Asia. If China did so in the Western Pacific, it could dominate the world's largest and most economically dynamic region. If Russia did so, it could fracture NATO and open Eastern Europe to Russian dominance.[209]

Colby is encouraged by the Pentagon's 2018 National Defense Strategy, which targeted Russia and China as the key U.S. adversaries, but there's a long way to go in putting its recommendations into force. Even if a full-scale war with either Russia or China remains unthinkable to most Americans, national security policymakers must prepare for it, and give us the tools

---

209   Colby, Elbridge. "How to Win America's Next War." *Foreign Policy*, 5 May 2019, https://foreignpolicy.com/2019/05/05/how-to-win-americas-next-war-china-russia-military-infrastructure/

to win it, should it be necessary. That is always the task of the Defense Department—to prepare the United States to prevail against threats. And as the Pentagon's strategy now makes clear, no threat is regarded as more serious than that represented by Russia and China.

To this end, then, as Colby sets out, the U.S. "must focus not on abstract metrics of its military superiority—such as how many carriers it puts to sea or how much it spends in comparison to other countries—but on its and its allies' clear ability to defeat major aggression in specific, plausible scenarios against a vulnerable ally or established partner such as Taiwan." Doing that will require dramatic changes. The Gulf War model, based on technological superiority, is obsolete, he argues—in no small part because Moscow and Beijing have been studying it for decades and have armed themselves to thwart it. The American military, as Colby sees it, "must shift from one that surges to battlefields well after the enemy has moved to one that can delay, degrade, and ideally deny an adversary's attempt to establish a fait accompli from the very beginning of hostilities and then defeat its invasion." To accomplish this will require a transformation of the military into a force that, "instead of methodically establishing overwhelming dominance in an active theater before pushing the enemy back, can immediately blunt the enemy's attacks and then defeat its strategy even without such dominance."

Colby also wants the U.S. to update its relationships with its allies. In this new era, the U.S. cannot do it all on its own anymore. The sooner the Americans and their European allies act on this realization, the better. Colby suggests that we encourage allies to specialize in areas that they excel at: so, for example, "front-line allies and partners such as Japan, Poland, Taiwan, and the Baltic states should concentrate on their ability to blunt Chinese or Russian attacks on their territory and to restrict Beijing's or Moscow's ability to maneuver through adjoining airspace and waterways by building their own A2/AD capabilities," while allies farther away from potential trouble spots, such as Australia or Germany, could "work on contributing, both through their forces and basing, to defeating Chinese or Russian aggression against nearby allies" and "partners such as France, Italy, and Spain with established interests in places such as North Africa should allocate more forces to handling secondary threats there."

I have cited Elbridge Colby's argument here at some length because I believe that it offers a compelling articulation for reorienting American military strategy and behavior. And I commend the Trump administration, in its National Security Strategy, for initiating the process that might make such a reorientation possible. But a high-level articulation is one thing; a full-scale, effective, and speedy implementation of a comprehensive strategy is another. Let us hope that officials in the Pentagon, and in the administration—whether Trump's or his successor's—are up to the task, because there is no time to lose.

Disentangling the Axis

Finally, there is the matter of addressing both Russia and China as separate players. In 2016, I published a book called *The Nixon Effect* that, among many other areas, examined Richard Nixon's legacy in our foreign policy—a big portion of which concerned his doings with Moscow and Beijing. What Nixon and Henry Kissinger were particularly good at was operating on multiple levels: making clear to the Soviets and Chinese that we were not friends, but also that we did not have to be mortal adversaries; that we could confront them when necessary, but when confrontation was not necessary, we could work with them—and at times play them off against one another.

As much as we are inclined—rightly—to see Russia and China moving closer together, and to view their challenge as a compound one, we must also remember that they remain sovereign states, proud cultures with long histories not only of independence but also deep-seated suspicion, even historical hatred, of the other. This alliance is not so entrenched that it cannot be weakened and eroded by shrewd American policymaking and diplomacy; more than enough suspicion and uncertainty exist on both sides.

We could and should, then, in the right contexts, attempt to peel Russia away from China by playing on Putin's insecurities about being the junior partner, about his insecurities (so far kept under wraps) about China's penetration into Central Asia with the Belt and Road, and about his bruised nationalist pride at seeing Beijing supplant Moscow as America's primary concern. And we could and should, in the right contexts, remind China, subtly, about the volatility of Russia's internal situation politically, about Moscow's egregious flaunting of international norms, and about its terribly weakened international economic clout.

Do the Chinese really want to be deepening their relationship with Moscow? How far do they want to go in that effort? Skilled American diplomats should raise such questions of both adversaries.

Nonetheless, however, and above all, we must not lose sight of the new environment in which we operate—one in which China and Russia have forged a closer, and more formidable, partnership than most observers ever thought possible. We simply must prepare for the possibility of a growing, and even formalized, Russia-China alliance. I'm still struck by how many prominent commentators dismiss its importance. The *New York Times* editorial board, for example, has consistently down-played the evidence of Moscow and Beijing's growing collaboration and convergence of interests.

This is foolhardy. The evidence of the Russian-Chinese challenge is abundant and accumulating. It remains for the United States to respond to it. Our task is one that, crucially, we must not (and cannot) pursue alone. With Russian adventurism in mind, we must do everything we can to strengthen our alliances with our European partners—a task that Trump, regrettably, has often approached with disinterest or outright scorn. Keeping in mind the even broader adventurism of China—a sweeping global vision of economic and military dominance—we must rally all freedom-minded nations to a stalwart resistance against Beijing's many weapons of warfare, whether military belligerence or economic colonization, and especially our Asian partners, who want American support in countering Chinese bullying and coercion.

Reawakening America

Again, I wrote this new book as a warning—yet another—to the United States about the global threat posed to our country to all democratic nations by the China/Russia axis. As I said in my introduction, I believe the last half-decade has more than proved out the arguments that I (and some others) have been making. We still face the need to get the American people fully cognizant of this threat and the challenges it poses.

I am doubly concerned about the threat not only because of the chaotic state of the world in 2020—with a pandemic as yet unresolved, and with America facing extraordinary social tensions and considerable breakdown of civic order—but also because, for years now, the power of the American idea has been eroding. The belief that the United States stands for the principles of freedom, liberty, and democracy seems often to evoke as much scorn as assent among our elites and a considerable portion of our population. That's not a hopeful sign in a world challenged profoundly by the resurgence of authoritarianism around the world, both as a system of governance and as an ideological conviction. It is not just democracy as a system of governance that has eroded in recent years, as Freedom House has documented; it is democracy as an idea. In our own country, we hear increasingly that the American system, and American history itself, is illegitimate; overseas, we concede enormous rhetorical ground to despotism and authoritarianism, no longer confident in asserting the force of democracy.

I have believed in American exceptionalism for my entire life—and I still do. Part of that instinct is a rejection of pessimism. However, what I've seen in recent years of Chinese and Russian advances, on the one hand, and American dysfunction, on the other, makes me more concerned than I've ever been. I hope, as I have hoped before, that the deepening seriousness of our circumstances, both domestically and abroad, will awaken American policymakers and citizens to the challenges that we face.

"Our struggle," I wrote in an earlier book, "is fundamentally about how we see ourselves. We have lost a unified national conviction that the American way is worth celebrating and defending, that democracy is the best form of government, and that America is rightly engaged with the world in defense of others who share these convictions. We must articulate this uniquely American vision again, both for our own sake and for the benefit of those around the world looking to America for leadership. Standing up to Russia and China and countering the corrosive impact of their antidemocratic message is central to regaining our national strength—and vital to the peace and security of the world."

These words are truer today than when they were written. In the final analysis, it is American resolve that will prove indispensable. Without a firm American commitment to countering this new force in international affairs, the reach and influence of the Moscow-Beijing axis will continue to grow—with grave consequences for freedom, democracy, and human rights around the world.

America Divided

I N LATE MAY AND JUNE 2020, THE UNITED STATES SAW scenes not observed since the late 1960s: mass protests, in cities around the country; mass rioting, in dozens of cities, with fires and violence and property destruction; looters smashing the windows of businesses and running off with merchandise, mobs fighting with police, and fires and smoke visible for miles.

The trouble began in Minneapolis, in response to the death of George Floyd, a black man who died after a police officer kept his knee on his neck for nearly nine minutes, while Floyd, face down on the pavement, protested more than once that he couldn't breathe. The heartless cruelty of Floyd's death, entirely avoidable with a modicum of humane policing, enraged thousands of Minneapolis citizens, who took to the streets in protest. The protests soon spun out of control, leading to wholesale rioting, looting, and destruction—and even the storming of a police precinct house, which was torched, without intervention by the city's mayor.

Trouble followed in dozens of other American cities, including New York, Philadelphia, Detroit, Los Angeles, Chicago, and

St. Louis. In New York, the windows of flagship stores on Fifth Avenue were smashed and their merchandise stolen.

Even the nation's capital was not spared. St. John's Church, across the street from the White House, was set aflame, and President Trump was directed, briefly, into the presidential bunker for his safety. Smaller outbreaks of disorder broke out in dozens of other cities. For about a week, it seemed that the United States stood on the precipice of a wholesale urban rebellion, as the nation's oldest curse—race relations—roared to life again. The lawless behavior that occurred in certain cities was indefensible, but the remorse and anger that dominated the public mood nationally was genuine and understandable. The Floyd episode was so stark in its disregard for human life that it shocked many into recognizing the deep-seated anger of the black community about many past incidents of such police violence. In such a climate, it was not surprising that concerns would be raised anew about racism in American society and fresh calls made to reckon with it.

With the passage of time, however, it became clear that this new momentum against racism was moving too far away from traditional American values of inclusion, assimilation, and equality. Ibram X. Kendi's bestselling *How to Be an Antiracist* attacked these same values, arguing that only a policy of societal reparations and intense racial consciousness could produce anything close to an equitable and fair society. A climate of mounting censoriousness prevailed in the media, as when journalists at the *New York Times* forced out the op-ed page editor for running an opinion piece by Senator Tom Cotton arguing that President Trump should invoke the Insurrection Act to put down urban rioting. And around the country, protesters took to pulling down statues and monuments of American historical figures deemed racist—not just leaders of the old Confederacy but also Founding Fathers from Thomas Jefferson to George Washington.

One thing was clear: regardless of how one viewed the protests, the rioting, or the statue-toppling, the United States was more polarized and divided than at any time in at least half a century—and totally lacking in common purpose. This reality weakens all of us, no matter what our political views.

And this weakness has real consequences, not only for our well-being as a nation but also in the context of the broader world, which remains as daunting as ever—and demanding, as ever, of real responses to real challenges.

Beijing and Moscow watched America's anguish with relish and satisfaction.

China wasted little time in seizing on the unrest in American cities to lambaste the United States for its recent support for Hong Kong protesters. "I want to ask Speaker Pelosi and Secretary Pompeo," said Hu Xijin, editor of the state-owned *Global Times*, "Should Beijing support protests in the U.S., like you glorified rioters in Hong Kong?"

Upping the ante, Hua Chunying, a spokeswoman for the Chinese Foreign Ministry, tweeted: "I can't breathe."[210] The derisive quotation echoed that uttered by the Black Lives Matter protest movement, a phrase that recounts what several victims of police brutality in the U.S. have been heard to say.

How can China not see the current anguish in the United States as a rich opportunity, not only for propaganda points but

---

210   Kirka, Danica. "World alarmed by violence in US; thousands march in London." AP, 31 May 2020,   https://www.yahoo.com/news/world-uneasily-watches-us-protests-130003544.html

also for more tangible gains? Remember, again, that the battle we're in involves more than just combating Chinese provocations in the South China Sea or Hong Kong or North Korea; more than negotiating favorable trade deals or securing better military alliances. It involves, in the final analysis, a battle between competing models of governance and ideological systems—between democratic societies and authoritarian ones.

It's why I consider this current struggle a new Cold War. And the social unrest and lack of national purpose in the United States are weapons in that battle for our adversaries. For the champions of authoritarian dictatorships like the one in Beijing, American chaos allows them to expose what they see as American hypocrisy, the disconnect between our lofty ideals and our more problematic reality; to divert critical attention to the Western world's failings, and away from the more egregious ones of authoritarian societies; and to undermine the convictions of the people of the United States, and the West more generally, making them less likely to defend their own systems—and maybe even to suggest, as some do, that systems like China's are superior. China casts a long shadow over our national life today.

Vladimir Putin's shadow may be somewhat smaller, comparatively, but we shouldn't forget his own role in our current dislocations. In June 2020, as American states and cities struggled to reopen, at least partially, news reports offered a fresh reminder of Putin's treachery: U.S. officials had uncovered evidence that Russia had been paying bounties to Taliban militants to kill American troops in Afghanistan.

And no one should be surprised that Putin, like the Chinese, had thoughts that he wished to share on America's 2020 domestic turmoil. In mid-June, as the United States continued to be roiled in unrest, and tension, from mass protests to statue topplings to the seizing of a section of Seattle by anarchists, Putin weighed in, telling an interviewer with state-owned Rossiya television that America's chaos was "a sign of some deep-seated internal crises."

The unrest in America, the Russian leader said, suggested a country splitting into pieces, lacking cohesion. "I think the problem is that group interests, party interests are put higher than the interests of the whole of society and the interests of the people. The president says we need to do such-and-such but the governor somewhere tells him where to go," he said, describing Trump's inability to exert his will on often-hostile governors or mayors in the U.S. Putin saw that situation—the messiness of American democracy, really—as a weakness, as he always has. He doubted whether, in Russia, "anyone in the government or the regions would say 'we're not going to do what the government says, what the president says, we think it's wrong.'"

No doubt, in Putin's authoritarian Russia, such scenarios don't arise too often.

Putin's words were calm and seemingly dispassionate, but devastating nonetheless, as when, commenting on the riots in U.S. cities, he said: "If this fight for natural rights, legal rights, turns into mayhem and rioting, I see nothing good for the country." And finally, just for good measure, Putin also added that Russia's battle against the coronavirus seemed to be going much more successfully than America's. Russia was "exiting the coronavirus situation steadily with minimal losses, God willing"—but "in the States it isn't happening that way."[211]

------

211   Wheaton, Sarah. "Putin: Protests and coronavirus show US 'internal crises'." Politico, 15 June 2020,   https://www.politico.eu/article/putin-protests-and-coronavirus-show-us-internal-crises/

More broadly, Putin's influence on the United States' current domestic unraveling should not be underestimated. Consider the influence of the Russian hacking of the 2016 presidential elections—not so much on the outcome itself, which intelligent people can still argue about. Did Russian involvement tip the election to Trump? Perhaps. Perhaps not.

But as I've written before: it doesn't matter. Granted, Hillary Clinton wouldn't see it that way. Democrats generally wouldn't see it that way. But from the Russian perspective, and from the perspective of the broader welfare of the United States, it doesn't matter—because Russia achieved its goal in any case.

That goal is destabilizing the United States, in no small part by delegitimizing another of its beleaguered institutions: its system of free and fair elections. Even before the Russian hacking scandal broke out, Americans' faith in their election process was waning; the Russian scandal has only weakened this faith further. In February 2020, 59 percent of respondents to a Gallup poll said that they were not confident about the honesty of the country's elections. That is an astonishing result in a nation once known as "the arsenal of democracy."

And Russia's use of trolls and "fake news" plants has soured millions of Americans on another institution: the news media. Gone is any illusion of faith among the American people in the honesty and integrity and reliability of news. People don't know what to believe anymore, and with a president who, himself, brands as "fake news" any story or report that he doesn't like, this tendency among the electorate is only heightened. The result is a populace that is essentially postmodern in its belief that truth lies in the eye of the beholder.

Vladimir Putin has had much to do with forging this effect on the minds of Americans.

"President Trump talks about winning? Right now, Putin is winning," said former Homeland Security secretary Tom Ridge in March 2017. Ridge was talking about the investigations in Washington of Putin's election meddling. Putin's goal, Ridge said, was "destabilization," what he described as "Let's create chaos, let's create uncertainty, let's destabilize the political environment." As Ridge saw it then, Moscow was succeeding in these efforts. "[The Russians] have done a wonderful job. If that was their goal, they have done it."[212] Nothing has changed since then to alter that judgment.

This erosion of faith in American institutions not only weakens America in a broad sense. It also empowers democracy's authoritarian adversaries—not just in Moscow but also in Beijing.

The reason? It relativizes differences between systems that, for generations, Americans saw as distinct as night is from day. That's not so true anymore. The more decline Americans see; the more corruption and dysfunction; the more delegitimization of the institutions of a free society—the media, elections, education, business—the more the authoritarian models of countries like Russia and China don't look so dramatically different. One of Putin's enduring implicit messages is: Your system is as corrupt as mine. And Donald Trump has even reinforced that message from time to time, shrugging off interviewers' questions about Putin's repressions with a rejoinder: We all do it.

---

212   Perkins, Madeleine Sheehan. "Former Homeland Security chief: 'Trump talks about winning — right now, Putin is winning'." Business Insider, 23 Mar. 2017,   http://www.businessinsider.com/tom-ridge-trump-putin-russia-2017-3

That isn't true. We're not equivalent. The truth remains that a world of difference—in principle, in morality, and in human liberty and flourishing—separates the democratic system of the United States (and its Western allies) from those of the authoritarian Axis of Russia and China. Failures and all, problems and all, America remains the world's best hope for the rule of law, the expansion of human liberty, and the preservation of democracy and what Thomas Paine called "the rights of man." Russia and China pose the greatest threat to that project. Only America can stop them.

And America can only do that if it believes in itself again. We must start there.

About the Author

Douglas Schoen has been one of the most influential Democratic campaign consultants for over forty years.

A founding partner and former principal strategist for the internationally known polling and consulting firm Penn, Schoen and Berland, he is also a founding partner of Schoen Cooperman Research, and he is widely recognized as one of the innovators of the modern polling and research business.

His political clients include former President Bill Clinton as well as former New York City Mayor Michael Bloomberg. He has worked for a number of United States senators and governors, in particular former Indiana Senator and Governor Evan Bayh, and a number of leading American corporations including Time Warner, Procter & Gamble and AT&T. Internationally, he has worked for the heads of states of over 15 countries, including British Prime Minister Tony Blair, Italian Prime Minister Silvio Berlusconi, and Israeli Prime Minister Menachem Begin.

He is the author of multiple books including *Putin's Master Plan: To Destroy Europe, Divide NATO, and Restore Russian Power and Global Influence and The Nixon Effect: How Richard Nixon's Presidency Fundamentally Changed American Politics.* In Schoen's latest book, entitled *Putin on the March,* he writes about how Russian President Vladimir Putin's mission to expand Russian influence around the world, destabilize the Western alliance, and delegitimize the very principles of free societies, has pursued with far more successes than setbacks.

Schoen is a regular contributor to the *Wall Street Journal,* the *Washington Post* and various other newspaper and online publications. He was a *Fox News* contributor for over 15 years. Schoen is a graduate of Harvard College, he has a Doctorate of Philosophy in Politics from the University of Oxford, and he is a graduate of Harvard Law School.

High Praise for Douglas E. Schoen

Collapse

"A remarkably comprehensive analysis of the challenges—internal and external—that we face today. Schoen is able to write intelligently about domestic and international issues alike, weaving them into one worrisome picture of the world… *Well worth reading.*"

—FAREED ZAKARIA, host of CNN's *Fareed Zakaria GPS*

"A seasoned veteran of political combat, he has advised presidents, prime ministers, governors, and mayors for decades… Part professor, part hard-nosed political adviser, Schoen is the perfect tutor at the perfect time."

—RICHARD PLEPLER, Former Chairman and Chief Executive Officer of HBO

"… a bracing, authoritative, and lucid account of the geopolitical crisis that is now afoot… precisely the type of sensible, clear-headed analysis which is so badly needed in Washington today."

—GILLIAN TETT, U.S. Managing Editor, *The Financial Times*

Putin's Master Plan

"… Schoen argues convincingly that American leadership remains key to peace in Europe, as it has for over seventy years."

—JOHN BOLTON, former UN Ambassador, 27th National Security Advisor and bestselling author of *The Room Where It Happened*

America in the Age of Trump

"… a terrific read, engaging and richly sourced, a provocative take on big, controversial issues and on political leaders… especially powerful regarding the loss of trust in institutions."

—BOB SHRUM, Carmen H. and Louis Warschaw Chair in Practical Politics, USC

"… must reading for anyone interested in politics and governing or in the current dysfunction of our political system."

—ED ROLLINS, campaign manager, President Ronald Reagan, 1984